CLASSIC BEARS

CLASSIC BEARS

HOW TO MAKE 14 HEIRLOOM BEARS

·JULIA JONES·

ANAYA PUBLISHERS LTD

For Charlotte Brandrick and her brother George

First published in Great Britain in 1994 by Anaya Publishers Ltd,
Strode House, 44-50 Osnaburgh Street, London NW1 3ND

Designer: Clare Clements
Photographer: Jon Stewart
Front cover picture: Tim Hill
Stylist: Barbara Stewart
Artwork: Anthony Duke

British Library Cataloguing in Publication Data
Jones, Julia
Classic Bears: How to make 14 Heirloom Bears
I. Title
745.592

ISBN 1 85470 179 7

Typeset in Great Britain by Litho Link Ltd, Welshpool, Powys
Colour reproduction by J. Film Process, Singapore
Printed and bound by Dai Nippon Printing Co. Ltd, Hong Kong

Page 1: A rare Steiff teddy bear circa 1906.
Page 2 (opposite title page): Julia Jones' 1920s German Bear.
See pages 48 to 53 for instructions.
Page 3 (title page): Julia Jones' American Bear.
See pages 82 to 87 for instructions.

CONTENTS

INTRODUCTION

The earliest advertisement for teddy bears appeared in 1909. The Christmas novelty gift offered by Morrells of Oxford Street, London, that year was 'Old Mistress Teddy that lived in a shoe', together with twelve baby bears, a sledge, ladder and even some bottles and bowls, all packaged together in a large crimson shoe.

The wonderful, lovable, loyal and friendly teddy bear is probably one of the most enduring treasures of childhood. Even most adults would not be embarrassed to admit their secret fondness for an old, worn bear. Ever since teddy bears gained popularity in the early part of the century, they have appeared as mascots and talismans; going into battle with their owners, facing the stresses of examinations and featuring in countless songs, books and verse.

The teddy bear came into the world in 1903. Since its conception it has been made in all shapes, sizes and colours with numerous expressions and capable of a wide range of actions.

This book looks at the classic bear and how it has evolved over the years. On the following pages, bears reminiscent of early examples can be made using modern materials and traditional methods. No complex needlework skills are necessary to produce wonderful collectors' bears, just straightforward sewing techniques.

DEFINING A CLASSIC BEAR

A classic bear has well-defined characteristics. It has slightly curved paws, which taper at the ends. Its feet are long in relation to its overall height; to the purist this ratio is set at 5:1. High quality felt or velvet oval or triangular pads complete the feet. It either has no claws or ones stitched in black wool or cotton thread. Its head is rather small and triangular – it may or may not have a central gusset – with a long, pointed muzzle. Its head and limbs are invariably attached to its body with hardboard or cardboard discs and split pins. Black boot button eyes are the hallmark of a traditional bear, with a nose and mouth either embroidered with black thread or conveyed by an oval of black leather.

TEDDY BEAR HISTORY

Although there are numerous stories surrounding the birth of the bear, it is probably accurate to attribute the lovable teddy to two simultaneous sources: America and Germany.

The American tale is perhaps the most entertaining, although not strictly documented. Certainly, a Russian immigrant shopkeeper, Morris Michtom, conceived the idea for a cuddly bear after seeing the now famous cartoon of President Roosevelt refusing to shoot a tethered bear cub. As Michtom's wife was a skilled toymaker, she set about creating what we now refer to as a Michtom teddy (see page 36).

The legend runs that the enterprising Michtom sent one of her bears to the president with the request to name the bear 'teddy' after Roosevelt's first name, Theodore. The President allegedly consented and 'Teddy's bear' was born.

Meanwhile, in Germany a young seamstress had begun to make soft toys. The girl was Margarete Steiff and so popular were her designs that by the close of the 19th century, she had become firmly established as a leading toymaker. It was her nephew Richard who brought the idea

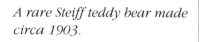

A rare Steiff teddy bear made circa 1903.

of a soft toy bear to Margarete's attention. Looking for a boy's alternative to the doll, Richard thought a bear might be the answer. After various modifications and some setbacks, the Steiff factory produced 'Friend Petz' in time for the Leipzig Toy Fair of 1903.

Evidently no one seemed interested in little Friend Petz until the last day of the Fair. Hermann Berg, an American buyer for a New York company, approached the Steiffs, complaining that there was little new or interesting that year. Richard showed him the small bear and it is said that he was so delighted he placed an order for 3,000.

And so the teddy bear had arrived. The new toy had such an impact that suppliers just could not keep up with demand. By the 1920s, and despite the interruption of World War I, firms in Britain had sprung up to manufacture these creatures. While US bears stayed more or less at home, German bears were exported around the world.

The shape of bears has evolved gradually over the years and makers have experimented with different colours, shapes and fabrics. The modern bear has mostly lost its jointed limbs and hump, and its body and face is rounder, but the basic appeal remains the same.

COLLECTING BEARS

Today, old bears have become most collectable and many are quite valuable. The main factors governing the price of a bear are its condition, quality, rarity value and desirability. In older bears look for the soft colours of old mohair (black being the exception), straw or wood wool stuffing and wooden boot button eyes which should be deeply set. The body should display a well-defined hump. As early bears were designed to stand on all fours, they should have long arms, extending half way down their legs.

Personal preferences for bears vary considerably from collector to collector. Only you can decide the style and decade which appeals most, but always beware of impulse buys. Check the facts before making a decision and determining a fair price. But when the choice has been made, make the most of the bear you have the privilege of owning!

MAKING BEARS

There is now a growing interest worldwide, not only for collecting bears but also making them in the traditional manner. On the following pages, you will find 14 bears – all with full patterns and clear instructions.

Even complete beginners will achieve remarkable success with their first bear by following the step-by-step instructions closely, while experienced bear-makers will find the useful tips contained throughout this book a stimulus to their creativity.

There is also scope to vary each bear, so that a tremendous range and variety of styles can be achieved, needing only a little imagination and confidence. Once the basic steps have been mastered, the desire to experiment will naturally develop. Making any bear and watching its personality develop as you work is rewarding and great fun.

However, when first making a particular bear, it is best to use the recommended fabric. Bears made up in different fabrics or colours will look quite unlike the ones illustrated. For the more experienced this can be one of the delights of making your own Classic Bears!

The classic bears in this book are not designed as toys for small children. If, however, one of them is to be made for a small child, it must conform to all toy safety standards.

Manufacturers were quick to realize the marketing potential of the endearing 'teddy' bear and over the years its form has appeared in the trademarks of many companies. Teddies have been used to promote all manner of produce, as widely diverse as ladies' hosiery, balloons and coal!

7

MATERIALS AND EQUIPMENT

Occasionally a nose moulded from leather or gutta-percha (a natural resin exuded from various Malaysian trees) can be found on a classic collectors' bear.

Classic bears have always been made from natural materials such as wool, mohair, angora and cashmere, with fillings of wood wool or straw. The eyes were almost always fashioned from black wooden boot buttons, though occasionally beads or metal discs were used. Most paw and foot pads were made from good quality felt. Other features, such as mouths and claws where included, were embroidered with simple stitches such as straight stitch, using cotton or wool embroidery threads.

During the world wars some resourceful people, faced with limited supplies of material, resorted to using sheepskin and surviving examples have a very unusual and distinctive look. A small number of early bears, with a somewhat unappealing appearance, were manufactured from 'burlap', a fabric coarsely woven from jute. This gave a hairless and slightly abrasive feel to a creature primarily designed to be cuddled.

In this section, the more recognizable and ubiquitous materials are described, together with the essential tools, equipment, materials and fittings required to make authentic collectors' bears today.

TOOLS AND EQUIPMENT

The following are all the simple tools and equipment you will need when making a classic bear using the techniques described in the section called Classic Bear-making. They are listed in the order in which they will be required.

Graph paper The pattern pieces on grids in this book are designed to be transferred to graph paper (or pattern paper) with 1in (2.5cm) squares. Should you wish to reduce or enlarge the size of a bear, you can use smaller or larger sized squared paper.

Tracing paper Ideally use a heavy-weight tracing paper for transferring the pattern outlines when making templates. Do not be tempted to economise by buying a lighter weight tracing paper as this may distort slightly or tear during use.

Never use ballpoint pens when marking templates of pattern pieces, as they will leave a mark which may be transferred accidentally to the right side of the fabric and will be impossible to remove.

Pencils A selection of hard and soft lead pencils are needed for making the pattern-piece templates and also for marking fabric. In many cases, a soft lead pencil will seem the most suitable choice for marking fabrics.

A French curve This is a flexible plastic rod which may be helpful in joining the marks smoothly when drawing pattern-piece shapes on graph paper.

Masking tape Masking tape is used to hold the tracing paper in position while the outlines are transferred to the templates.

Non-smudge ink pen When marking templates with a pen, it is essential to use one that will not smudge.

When marking dark fabrics for bear-making, coloured pencils or chalk can be used.

Card Thin white modelling card or cardboard is needed for making semi-permanent templates which can be used many times. Any type of lightweight card can be used, provided it is clean and fairly stiff.

Craft scissors Short round-ended scissors are needed for cutting paper and card or cardboard.

Tailor's chalk and dressmaker's marker pens Both tailor's chalk and dressmaker's marker pens are useful when marking fabric around the templates. Tailor's chalk is most suitable for dark fabrics and it will brush out easily after use. Dressmaker's marker pens are also used to label and mark fabric pieces. Usually pale blue in colour, they work well on most fabrics, but the manufacturer's instructions must be carefully followed to avoid leaving stains on some fabrics.

Dressmaking scissors Dressmaking scissors are used for cutting fur fabric, suedette, leather and, indeed, all other bear-making fabrics. Ideally, these should be 7–8in (18–21cm) long and have offset handles.

Embroidery scissors Fine-bladed, sharp embroidery scissors are useful for cutting around small pattern pieces, negotiating sharp angles and for all embroidery work.

Pins Long slim dressmaker's pins are required to hold seams together before tacking (basting). As an extra safety precaution, coloured glass-headed pins can be used. Either way, do count the number of pins used as you work and be sure to remove them all as soon as possible.

Sewing machine and needles Although it is perfectly possible to make any of the bears in this book without the aid of a sewing machine, it is assumed that most readers will have access to one and instructions are written accordingly. A ball-point or sharp sewing-machine needle can be used for fur fabrics, velvet and velveteens; and a wedge point for leather or suede. The machine needle size depends on the fabric thickness and a size 14 to 16 will suit most fabrics. A heavy-weight leather or suede will require a size 16 to 18.

Needles A variety of needles will be necessary for the various hand-sewing and embroidery techniques used to make a classic bear. Besides the obvious choice of sharps and embroidery needles for general work, it is necessary to use a 3in (7.5cm) darning needle which is slim enough not to snag or distort the fabric when inserting eyes. A toymaker's or packing needle is useful for ladder stitching openings after stuffing. Alternatively, a fine curved upholstery needle will serve equally well.

Seam ripper A seam ripper is useful for unpicking seams quickly to undo errors, but great care must be used not to tear or cut the fabric.

Fine crochet hook or bodkin Either a fine crochet hook or a bodkin can be used for teasing out pile trapped in machine-stitched seams. A knitting needle could also be used, but it is likely to bend during use.

Stiletto or awl A stiletto (or awl) is used for making holes in fur fabric or card templates. However, if this is not available, a fine knitting needle can be used instead.

A stuffing stick A strong stick is necessary to ensure that any filling medium can be tightly packed into even the smallest corners. A cheap alternative to a custom-made stuffing stick can be made from an 8in (20cm) length of ⅜in (1cm) dowelling, smoothly sanded before use. Stuffing sticks can also be used to assist in the turning of small limbs and the pushing out of noses and feet. Orange (manicure) sticks are useful when working on tiny bears.

Tape measure A tape measure is needed for measuring the positions for eyes, ears and nose.

Do not be tempted to cut paper with dressmaking or embroidery scissors, as this will quickly blunt their blades.

'T' pins are useful for holding bear ears in position before stitching.

Any hand-stitched seams in bear-making must be very accurately and firmly worked to withstand the pressure exerted during the stuffing process.

The handle of a wooden spoon or a chopstick could be used as stuffing stick in bear-making.

Pliers are useful for flattening the wire on the back of some glass eyes, to aid their insertion through the fabric.

If any of the bears in this book is to be made for a child, it is essential that a suitable, non-flammable fabric is used.

As synthetic fur fabrics are much cheaper than natural fur fabrics, it may be wise for a beginner to practise with these first.

The mohair plush originally used by all German makers in the manufacture of their bears is believed to have been woven exclusively in Yorkshire, England.

Pliers Long-nosed pliers are essential for bending split pins when assembling crown joints and for pulling through a needle when extra purchase is required.

Wire cutters These are used for cutting the joining wire found on some glass eyes and for cutting through wrongly assembled joints in order to release them.

Teasel brush A teasel or soft bristle nail brush is useful to help ease trapped strands from machine-stitched seams or to fluff up the pile on a finished bear. On crushed mohair it is better to use a soft nail brush, rather than the wire teasel type, as this will not disturb the distinctive antique appearance of the fabric.

FABRICS AND THREADS

There are many types of fabric to choose from, both traditional and modern, and these can vary enormously in price and quality. The work entailed when making a classic bear demands that you use the best possible material, to produce an heirloom. Fur fabrics are either woven or knitted and the materials used for the pile may be synthetic or natural. Obviously, the choice for a classic bear would be for a natural and traditional material such as mohair, wool or cashmere.

Plush The word 'plush' is a term often applied to fur fabrics. This simply means that the fabric has a nap which is softer and longer than velvet. Plush is usually manufactured from silk, cotton or wool and will produce an authentic and lovable bear.

Synthetic furs Synthetic furs are usually produced with a knitted backing, which is not ideally suited to the production of a collectors' bear. Knitted fabrics do not withstand stress and are inclined to give and pull out of shape during stuffing, whereas natural fibres such as mohair, alpaca, silk and wool have a woven backing that will withstand pressure, resulting in a better quality and firmer bear.

The pile length of each type of fabric can vary considerably, as does its quality and softness, and these factors will also determine the look of your finished bear.

Two of the bears in this book – the 1950s British Bear and the 1940s American Bear have been made with man-made fabrics. Although both bears can, of course, also be made up using an alternative, natural fabric for a more traditional appeal. If you have never made a soft toy before, use a good quality synthetic fabric and follow the step-by-step classic bear instructions carefully to produce results that should be very satisfying. Keep in mind the possibility of stretching, however, when the stuffing stage is reached.

Non-pile fabrics The patterns in this book can be also used for a modern approach to bear-making, using techniques such as quilting or patchwork and fabrics such as silk, cotton or linen. A good-quality German felt can also be used to produce a hairless bear, but in this case avoid any pattern with a very thin body, arms or legs, as the bear's thinness will be accentuated by its lack of fur!

Mohair pile fabrics Classic teddies were and still are, in general, made from mohair fabric. This is obtained from the coat of the Angora goat, which is woven into soft luxurious fabric. The process of making mohair fabrics for bears can take as long as six weeks and this explains their relatively high cost. A mohair substitute, made from a mixture of wool and cotton, is obtainable.

Fur fabric widths Fur fabric is generally woven in widths of 54in (137cm) and a 16in (41cm) bear would require ½yd (45cm) of this. If you intend to make several bears, it is possible, by careful placing of the pattern pieces, to economise on fabric, cutting several from 1yd (91cm). Different widths of fabric will, of course, need differing lengths. If in doubt, cut a sheet of paper to the required width and arrange the templates on this, measuring the depth of fabric required to cut them all satisfactorily.

Felt Traditional bears always had felt paw and foot pads, usually of beige, black or cream. Felt is easily and quickly cut and has no pile or right and wrong side. Consequently, pattern pieces can be fitted jigsaw-like onto the fabric resulting in very little waste.

To the right are some fur fabrics currently available for classic bear-making. Also shown are fabrics used for pads, such as felt and suedette.

The felt used for classic bear paws should always be the best quality. Today the best felt is manufactured in Germany.

Velveteens and Velvets Velveteen was used for paws and pads for many bears in the period from 1910 to 1940. It is a cotton pile fabric, similar in appearance to velvet, but with a much shorter nap or pile. Because velveteen is harder to find today, velvet is often used in its place on classic bears.

Suede and leather Ovals for noses, paw and foot pads can be cut from suede or leather. The most usual colours are light beige, brown or black. Old, worn gloves can be successfully recycled for this purpose. Suede could be used for any of the bear pads in this book.

Suedette This fabric is manufactured to resemble suede. It can be purchased in a variety of colours and is extremely easy to cut and sew.

Threads All-purpose sewing thread (no. 30) of the same colour as the fabric is required for machine stitching classic bears. In addition, a heavy-duty or buttonhole thread is required for some sewing jobs such as attaching the eyes and ears securely; or for machine stitching large bears, or heavy-weight leather or suede. Cotton or wool embroidery threads are the most suitable choices for embroidering features.

BEAR FILLING OR STUFFING

Wood wool was traditionally used for the heirloom bears and most modern collectors' bears are still stuffed with it. Occasionally referred to as 'Excelsior', wood wool is made of long, thin fine-quality wood shavings. Kapok, sometimes called 'silk cotton', took over from wood wool as the most popular medium for stuffing toys from the 1940s until the advent of man-made fibres.

Kapok This is a natural material similar to cotton, and is formed from the short fibres which surround the seeds of a tropical tree. If you are stuffing a large bear with kapok remember that it is relatively heavy, and it may be advisable to combine kapok, with some other medium. Asthma sufferers are advised to wear a mask when using kapok, as the fine strands and dust can prove irritating.

Sheep's wool This can be collected from hedges and barbed wire fences or bought in a fleece. With careful washing it will make a wonderful filling material and can be teased out gently to fill tiny corners. As it is possible to contract a skin complaint from unwashed sheep's wool, it is advisable to wear rubber gloves while collecting and washing. Do make sure that wool prepared at home is thoroughly dry before use.

Wood wool This can be ordered from specialist suppliers (see page 112) and will usually be packaged in a polythene bag or sack. As soon as it is delivered, it should be emptied into a large cardboard box or wooden tea chest, as storage in polythene may cause dampness and rotting.

Wood wool is sold in a semi-compressed state and the blocks should be lightly teased out to their full volume just before use. Check carefully and remove any large wood shavings, before beginning to stuff a bear.

For a smooth finish paws, feet and muzzles should be stuffed with a small amount of synthetic filling to give a softer feel, before completing the stuffing using wood wool.

Man-made fibres A variety of man-made fibres are available for soft toy making – the most commonly used is polyester or terylene (Dacron). When purchasing it is essential to specify whether a soft or firm fill is required for the bear in question. Terylene produces a loose, open and

Embroidery threads such as stranded cotton (floss) or pearl cotton are often used for embroidering the features on contemporary collectors' teddy bears.

Turn to page 112 for a list of specialist suppliers who sell classic bear fabrics, fittings, and filling or stuffing.

When buying any filling or stuffing sold for soft toys, always read the labelling on the packaging so that you are aware of the safety standard information.

fairly resilient stuffing medium, while polyester has less crimp and will need slightly more to produce the same results.

Foam rubber Never be tempted to use the brightly coloured pieces of foam rubber sold in some stores as a suitable medium for stuffing good quality toys. Although it has the advantage of being cheap, readily available and hygienic, it also has a nasty habit of sticking to the inside of the fabric and will make the finished bear very heavy and shapeless.

BEAR FITTINGS

The fittings used for classic bears – such as eyes, joints and growlers – can be purchased from specialist suppliers (see page 112). Remember that the bear instructions in this book are for traditional collectors' bears which are not suitable for small children. If you intend to make toys for children, strict safety regulations must be adhered to and only fittings which comply with these regulations can be used.

Eyes Following tradition, all classic bears made for the collector's market are fitted with boot button or glass eyes. A careful search through boxes of odds and ends at antique and bric-à-brac fairs will sometimes be rewarded by discovering wooden boot button eyes. Failing that, specialist suppliers sell reproduction boot button eyes in sizes ranging from ¼in (7mm) to ⅝in (16mm).

Safety eyes, made of plastic, can be found in handicraft shops or mail order catalogues. They range in size from ⅜in (9 mm) to 1¼in (45mm) and are made in various colours, including amber, brown and black. It is possible to purchase a special tool to help to exert pressure when assembling safety eyes. It is not essential, however, as an empty sewing cotton spool can be employed in much the same manner.

Joints Most classic bears are assembled using crown joints. These come in different sizes. Bears made for children must be fitted with the correct safety-locking plastic joints.

Growler boxes This can be fitted to most bears to provide a voice. A growler is made from a cylindrical cardboard container with holes at one end like a pepper pot. It has a weight inside which, when the bear is tipped backwards, presses on a small bellows, forcing air through its reed to produce a sound similar to a short growl. These teddy bear 'voices' were introduced in 1908, but were later replaced with cheaper, mass produced 'squeakers'.

It is wise to purchase a growler from a specialist bear supplier. Otherwise, do listen to its sound carefully – you may find that your bear sounds more like a cow or a duck!

Squeakers A squeaker comprises a small bellows, which, when pressed, forces air through a reed, emitting a high-pitched note.

Tinklers A tinkler is a simple device made from a cardboard cylinder containing steel pins of various lengths. A weight is suspended from one end and when the cylinder is rolled, this hits the pins, making a soft tinkling sound.

Musical boxes Musical boxes were first included in bears during the 1920s, when, understandably, the tune 'Teddy Bears' Picnic', was a popular choice. Today, musical boxes suitable for insertion in soft toys are enclosed in a small tin and have a key for winding which is fitted to a screw. (See page 27 for inserting a musical box in a teddy bear.)

Never use any fittings either outside or inside a teddy bear that is to be given to a child unless these fittings comply with toy safety regulations.

Growlers, tinklers and musical boxes can only be inserted into bears big enough to accommodate them. Bears containing any of these items should be well stuffed with wood wool.

CLASSIC BEAR-MAKING

The traditional techniques for making classic bears are outlined here in these detailed step-by-step instructions. Before making any of the bears featured in this book, you will need to read this chapter. Where a bear has a special feature not included in these general directions, the necessary techniques are outlined in the individual instructions.

The pattern pieces for the Miniature Bear and the 1980s Bear are given actual size (see pages 54 and 100).

PREPARING THE TEMPLATES

The first stage in the process of bear-making is preparing the pattern-piece templates. The pattern pieces for most of the bears in this book have been drawn on a grid with squares representing 1in (2.5cm). These pieces must be transferred onto graph paper with 1in (2.5cm) squares, then onto tracing paper and finally onto the thin, stiff template card or cardboard. To make a bigger or smaller bear than the recommended one, a graph paper with different sized squares can be used. The pattern pieces can also be reduced or enlarged on a photocopier.

1 To transfer the pattern shapes to graph paper, first note where each curved line crosses the sides of a square. Make a light mark at these points on the graph paper before drawing in the finished curves. An artist's flexible plastic rod may be helpful in joining the marks smoothly. When all the shapes have been transferred to graph paper, transfer all pattern markings, labels and, most importantly, the name of the bear.

2 Trace each pattern shape onto tracing paper, using a soft lead pencil and a firm hand. Transfer all pattern markings in the same way. Turn over the tracing paper and lay it over a piece of card or cardboard, securing it with masking tape. Using a hard lead pencil, go over the traced outlines and markings, thus transferring them to the card. Repeat this process for each pattern shape, fitting the pieces closely together.

3 Set aside the tracing paper and, using a fine non-smudge pen, reinforce the traced lines and markings on all of the templates. Still using the pen, insert all remaining labels. Then cut out each template, using craft scissors. Cut smoothly and accurately, as the quality of the templates will affect the quality of your bear. Using a stiletto, push holes through templates at all dart points and at the positions for arm and leg joints.

TRANSFERRING PATTERN SHAPES TO FUR FABRIC

Before beginning to outline the pattern shapes onto your fur fabric, first check that you have the required number of templates. (You will notice that your templates are mirror images of the shapes in the book because the tracing paper was turned over to transfer the pieces to the template cardboard.)

The type of fabric from which each pattern piece is to be cut is clearly marked on each piece. How many pieces to cut from a template and whether to reverse a piece (for a right and left side) is also indicated. All this should be checked carefully after the pieces have been drawn, but before cutting, paying attention to the direction of the pile.

The minimum amount of fabric required for each bear is given in the Materials list accompanying each set of instructions. If more material has to be purchased than is necessary to cut a particular bear, it may be possible, by careful arrangement of the pattern pieces, to cut a second smaller bear from the surplus. In any event, do not throw the remnants and scraps away. These can be stored, for future use.

It may be necessary to try various layouts to achieve the most economical use of fabric, but experience will quickly make this apparent. It is not possible, as with dress patterns, to work on folded fabric, cutting two pieces at a time. You must therefore remember to reverse the template in order to form 'pairs' of pattern pieces where necessary.

Most of the patterns in this book require two body sections, two side head sections, one head gusset, as well as two inner arms, two outer arms, two inner legs, two outer legs, two paw pads and two foot pads. The paw and foot pad pieces will be cut from suedette, leather, velvet or felt as instructed.

Do not use a ballpoint pen to mark any fabric. It may smudge and would undoubtedly stain the material, which could spoil the finished bear. Note that all seam allowances are included in the templates.

Using templates (instead of paper patterns) allows for more accurate bear-making. Templates can also be re-used many times.

When fur fabric or velvet is stroked, the pile or 'nap' lies smoothly or it ruffles, depending on the direction in which it lies. The pile on a bear should always run downwards from head to toe, except on the top of the muzzle and the ears. If in any doubt check the direction in which the fur runs on a dog or cat!

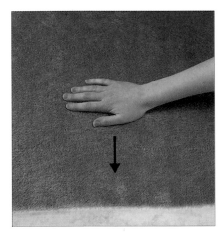

1 First spread the fur fabric out on a large flat surface (such as a table or a clean floor), face up. Check the direction of the nap or pile by stroking the fur flat, noting the direction it runs.

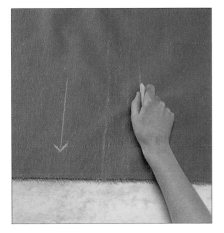

2 Turn the fur fabric face down, so that the pile of the fur runs towards you. Then carefully draw a few large arrows showing the direction of the fur pile, using tailor's chalk.

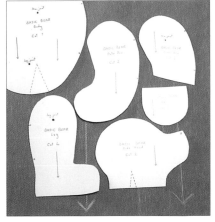

3 Arrange the templates on the fabric, being sure to match the directional arrows to the direction of the pile. Pattern pieces should always be cut on a single layer of fur fabric.

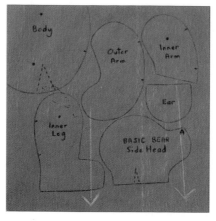

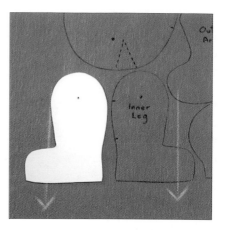

4 When you have decided on the layout, you can begin tracing the shapes. Carefully holding each template firmly in place with one hand, draw around the edge of each template, using tailor's chalk, a marker pen or a soft lead pencil.

5 Transfer onto the fabric all markings for openings, arm and leg joint positions, dart points, seam labels and any notches. Then label each piece with the part name, e.g. 'inner arm', 'leg', 'head gusset', 'paw pad', 'body', etc.

6 Prepare remaining pieces in the same way, reversing templates where necessary so that there is a 'right' and 'left' side of head or an 'inner' and 'outer' arm, etc. After completion, check that you have the correct number of cut pieces.

CUTTING FABRICS

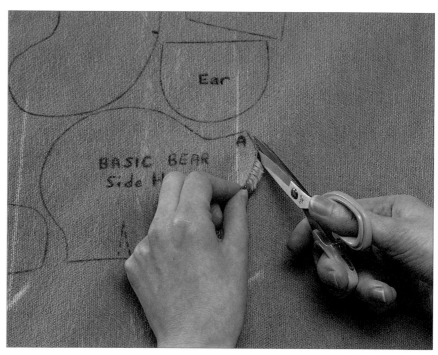

Remember that the seam allowances are already included inside the pattern-piece outlines.

When absolutely sure that the pattern pieces are drawn correctly, lay the fabric right side down on a firm surface. Then using sharp, pointed dressmaking scissors, push the point through the fabric and carefully cut out each drawn shape. Rather than cutting through both the fabric and the fur pile, try to cut only the ground fabric, leaving the fur to be teased apart. On small or complex shapes, it may be easier to use sharp, embroidery scissors.

As each piece is cut, check that it is correctly labelled and that all necessary instructions have been transferred. As you work, place all the cut pieces in a clean self-seal plastic bag or a paper bag, keeping identical pieces together.

Your bear's velvet, suedette or leather foot and paw pads should be traced onto the wrong side of the fabric in the same way as the pattern pieces were transferred to the fur, taking the direction of the nap into account in the case of the velvet. Felt has no right and wrong side and the shapes can be transferred to either side of felt.

Using small, sharp scissors, cut very carefully around each paw and foot pad shape being sure to keep closely to the outlines.

It may be advisable, when using especially soft fabrics, to cut paw and foot pads out again in a medium weight interfacing, which can then be tacked (basted) to the outer fabric to give additional body.

SEWING THE PATTERN PIECES

As fur fabric has a habit of 'slipping', all pattern pieces should be pinned together first before tacking (basting), using long slim pins placed at right angles to the seams. After careful pinning, the pieces should be tacked (basted), using long running stitches. It is helpful to tuck the pile inwards between the two edges of fabric while tacking (basting).

If the pattern pieces do not fit exactly, use pins and tacking (basting) stitches to ease the longer edge gently before machine stitching. The dense pile of fur fabric can, fortunately, be used to cover a number of minor mishaps! This does not mean, however, that anything but the greatest care should be taken when stitching, as the ultimate character of your bear will be affected by your attention to detail.

When machine stitching, added strength can be given to a seam by turning the fabric and running a second row of stitches back along the original seamline. To secure the thread ends, always backstitch at the beginning and end of a machine-stitched seam.

All seam allowances are ¼in (7mm) on bears unless otherwise stated. References to the seamline apply to an imaginary line at this distance from the cutting edge.

In the instructions given for each bear, the word 'stitch' means pin, then tack (baste) and then machine stitch, unless the instructions state otherwise.

After each seam has been machine stitched, any pile trapped in the seams should be gently teased out using a bodkin or stiletto. (See also 'teasel brush' on page 10.)

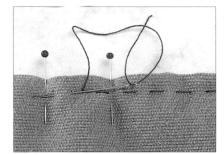

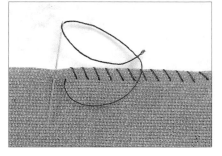

Running stitch is the simplest of the hand-stitching techniques used in bear-making. It is used for tacking (basting) and for stay stitching along some fur-fabric edges before the seams are machine stitched.

Ladder stitch is used for closing openings after stuffing. It is worked by taking a tiny stitch alternately on each side of the seam. After every few stitches the thread should be pulled firmly to close the seam.

Oversewing (overcast stitches) can be used along the raw edges of fabrics that are likely to fray. Never use oversewing stitches to close openings as they will form an ugly ridge, in which the stitches will show.

STITCHING THE BEAR'S HEAD

1 Some bear heads do not have shaping darts, but if there are any they may be stitched first before joining head pieces. Fold together the dart gusset of each side head section and pin. Tack (baste) outside the dart line from the tip of the dart to the fabric edge. Machine stitch the dart. Remove tacking (basting).

2 Do not slash darts, but press them down firmly (away from the muzzle) using a thumb and forefinger (index finger). Using heavy-duty thread, knotted and doubled, stay stitch along the lower neck edge with short, even running stitches. This will prevent the raw edge from stretching out of shape.

3 Place the side head sections right sides together and pin and tack (baste) the lower muzzle seam which goes from the tip of the nose to the neck. Machine stitch this seam, remembering to always start and finish each seam with a few backstitches. Remove tacking (basting) stitches.

4 If any darts appear on the head gusset pattern piece, stitch these in the manner described in Step 1. Using heavy-duty thread, stay stitch along the seamline on both long edges of the gusset. The fitting of the head gusset is critical for the finished head shape. Great care should be taken to make sure that the gusset does not stretch out of shape. (As you join the gusset, it may be helpful to turn the head right side out occasionally to check the balance and shape of the muzzle and head.)

5 Pin the head gusset to one side of the head, easing to fit where necessary. Make sure that the centre notch on the nose tip of the gusset is lined up accurately with the centre of the lower muzzle seam. When you are entirely satisfied with the fit and shape of the seam, tack (baste) the gusset and the side of the head together just inside the seamline, using small running stitches. The seam may need to taper towards the nose tip. Join on the second side of the head in the same way.

6 When completely satisfied with the easing and shaping of these seams, machine stitch from the point of the nose to the back neck edge on each side of the gusset, starting the machine stitching as close as possible to the muzzle seam on each side of the nose notch. Remove the tacking (basting) stitches and trim the seams around the nose to ⅛in (3mm) to ensure a smooth muzzle. (Be careful when trimming not to cut the seam.) Set the head section aside for stuffing later.

STITCHING THE BEAR'S BODY

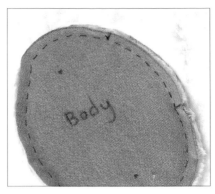

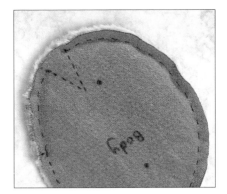

1 The bear body-shapes vary, and some have an upper and lower dart on each of the two body sections. Before joining the body pieces, stay stitch along the seamline of the back opening on each of the two pieces, using heavy-duty thread and small running stitches. Place the body sections right sides together, matching any notches. If there are no darts, simply pin, tack

(baste) and machine stitch body pieces together, leaving an opening for stuffing (above left). If there are body darts (above right), pin from the edges of the upper dart around to the edges of the lower dart. Tack (baste), then machine stitch centre front seam and centre back seam, each from dart to dart; leaving opening for stuffing. Remove tacking (basting).

Some bears have four body sections. In these cases, the side seams should be joined first to create a left and right body section. The general instructions can then be followed to complete the body.

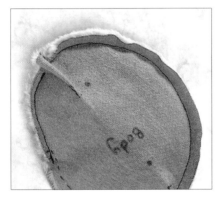

2 To complete a body with darts, flatten the top body section across the seamline, placing the top dart edges together. Pin and tack (baste) this dart from the farthest point to the seam edge. Remove the pins and machine, again starting from its farther point to the seam edge. Then remove tacking (basting) stitches. The tiny space left where the four seams meet will provide the hole for the bear's head joint.

3 Flatten the dart seam towards the back of the body, using the pressure from the thumb and forefinger (index finger). Do not be tempted to slash or cut these darts as this may seriously weaken the fabric. Pin, tack (baste) and machine stitch the dart at the lower body edge in the same way. As there are no joints to be attached here, try to make all machine stitching lines coincide as closely as possible. Set body aside for stuffing later.

Most of the bears have seam allowances of ¼in (7mm). Check individual instructions for seam allowances for the two smallest bears (pages 54 and 100).

19

ATTACHING PAW PAD TO INNER ARM

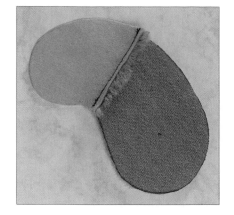

Unless great care is exercised, a smooth fabric such as suedette tends to slide across the surface of a fur fabric during the pinning and tacking (basting) processes.

1 Take an inner arm and a paw pad section and, with the right sides together, pin and tack (baste) along this seamline. Machine stitch and remove tacking (basting) stitches. Trim the seam close to the machine stitching and press the seam upwards towards the top of the arm, using the thumb and forefinger (index finger).

2 Tease the pile from the seamline using a bodkin or stiletto and brush the fur lightly. If using a teasel brush, avoid scratching or pulling the fabric of the paw. This is particularly important when using suede, leather or felt. (Only use a teasel brush if instructed.) Join the second inner arm and paw pad sections in the same way.

STITCHING THE BEAR'S ARMS

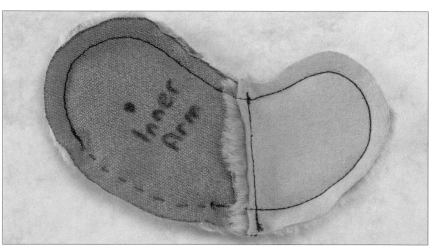

The finished seam between the paw pad and the arm should face upwards towards the top of the arm to prevent it showing through on the smooth surface of the paw.

Stay stitch the stuffing opening along the seamline on both the inner and outer arms. Place a front and back arm section right sides together, ensuring that the seamline of the paw is pressed upwards. Pin and tack (baste) all around the arm, leaving the stay-stitched edge open. Starting from the edge of the stuffing opening, machine stitch around the arm, paying particular attention to the paw seams. Trim the seams where necessary and turn the arm right side out. Tease any trapped pile from the seamline. Make the second arm in the same way and set both arms aside for stuffing later.

STITCHING THE BEAR'S LEGS

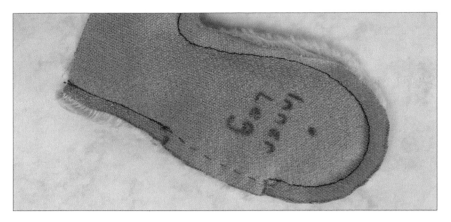

Stay stitch along the seamline of the stuffing opening on the inner and outer leg sections. Place these right sides together, and pin carefully, taking care to align each lower straight edge of the foot correctly. Tack (baste), then machine along the seamline around the leg section, leaving the lower edge and stuffing opening unstitched. Remove the tacking (basting) stitches. Turn the leg right side out and pull any trapped pile from the seamlines. Turn the leg inside out once more.

Before machine stitching, all stuffing openings on the bear pattern pieces are stay stitched using a heavy-duty sewing thread.

ATTACHING THE BEAR'S FOOT PADS

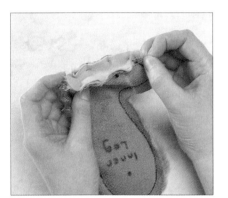

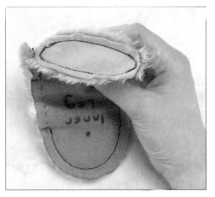

1 Place a foot pad within the oval formed by the lower straight edge of the foot, lining up the front and back notches with the front and back seam-lines. Pin the pad in position. It may be necessary to stretch the fur fabric slightly to take in the curve of the oval smoothly. Using very small running stitches, tack (baste) around the pad, trying to maintain its oval shape as far as possible. Tack (baste) each side of the foot separately, starting and ending at a seamline and leaving seam free.

2 Remove the pins and turn the leg right side out to check that the pad is correctly placed. When you are completely satisfied, turn the leg inside out and machine stitch the pad, again working each side of the foot separately and ending and starting stitching as close as possible to the seamlines. Remove the tacking (basting) stitches, turn the leg right side out and brush out the pile on all the seams. Make the second leg in the same way and set both legs aside for stuffing later.

The foot-pad seam is worked in two sections on either side of the leg seams to avoid having to stitch through two thicknesses of fur fabric. The foot-pad seam allowance is tapered as it approaches the leg seams.

BEAR EYES

Both plastic teddy-bear safety eyes and traditional glass or boot button eyes come in various sizes. Altering the size and position of the eyes will greatly alter the expression of the finished bear. For instance, large eyes will give a bright, wide-awake look to your bear. By careful positioning these can be made to give the impression of slight surprise. Whatever the size of the eyes, try out various positions before deciding, then mark the centre position of each eye using a glass-headed pin.

Glass and boot button eyes are inserted after the head has been stuffed (see opposite page), but safety eyes are inserted before the head is stuffed. For inserting safety eyes, turn the head right side out and make a tiny hole by easing the fabric threads aside with a stiletto or bodkin. Push the shank of the eye through to the wrong side. Then press down the securing washer over the shank as firmly as possible. It is possible to purchase a small strip of metal with two small holes, known as an 'eye tool' or 'flat safety tool' which will help to give additional pressure on the washer.

STUFFING THE BEAR'S HEAD

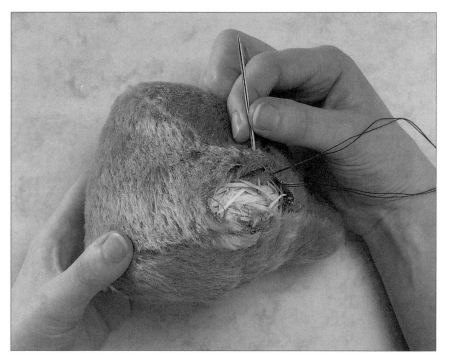

Begin by rolling a small amount of polyester filling between the palms of your hands to form a small ball. Then, using a stuffing stick, push the ball into the muzzle of the bear to begin to shape the nose section. Continue to fill the muzzle in this way, using your hands to mould and shape the bear from the outside. When the nose and muzzle are well shaped and firm, continue to stuff the head, using wood wool and working from the muzzle upwards, outwards and downwards. When sufficient filling has been added to the head, thread a darning needle with a doubled and knotted length of heavy-duty thread. Run this around the neck opening, using medium-length straight stitches. Do not fasten off the thread.

INSERTING THE NECK CROWN JOINT

  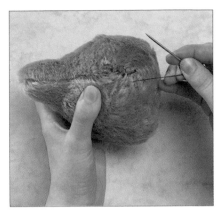

1 Assemble the first part of the larger crown joint by threading a washer and one hardboard disc on to the split pin. (While inserting the crown joint in Step 2, check that there is sufficient stuffing behind it to hold it securely in position when the neck opening is closed.)

2 Push the head of the split pin, the washer and the hardboard disc into the neck opening of the bear's head. The joint should sit above the line of running stitches. Take up the needle and heavy-duty thread and draw up the running stitches quite tightly, to hold the joint firmly in place.

3 Take long stitches backwards and forwards through the fur fabric and across the joint around the split pin. Pull these stitches tightly and secure with a few stitches, before cutting the thread. Pull the split pin firmly to ensure that its head is sitting against the enclosed hardboard disc.

FIXING GLASS OR BOOT BUTTON EYES

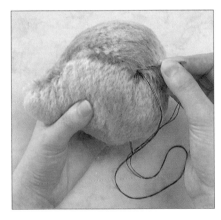 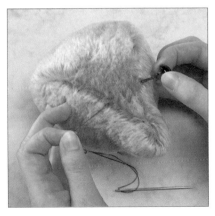 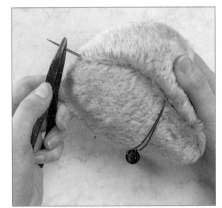

1 Before fixing the bear's eyes, determine the exact positions of eyes and ears. Thread a long darning needle or bodkin with a long, doubled length of heavy-duty thread, knotting this several times at the end. Take the needle through the head from the position of the left ear seamline to the position of the left eye, bringing the needle through the fabric and pulling the thread slightly to tighten the tension.

2 Using a stiletto, push aside the ground fabric warp and weft threads from around the needle thread, thus making a small hole through which the 'bail' or loop of the eye can be passed. Thread the first eye onto the needle and take it down the thread to push the 'bail' firmly through the fabric. Take the needle back through this hole and across the muzzle to surface at the position of the second eye.

3 Repeat the last step for the second eye, but finish by taking the needle through the head to the position of the seamline of the right ear. Tighten the thread to pull in both eyes, forming a slight depression in each to provide the eye socket. Anchor the thread firmly by making several small straight stitches in one place on the ear line and cut off the working thread close to the fabric.

STITCHING AND ATTACHING THE BEAR'S EARS

The ears are attached using oversewing (also called overcasting) stitches. Before stitching them in place, check that they are symmetrical and give the bear the right appearance.

Place two ear shapes right sides together. Pin, tack (baste) and machine stitch around the upper curve. Make the other ear in the same way and turn both right side out.

Then pin the back edge of each ear to the head. Using heavy-duty thread, stitch from the centre point of one ear to the outer edge, using small oversewing (overcast) stitches pulled tightly. At the outer edge, tuck in the seam edges and stitch them inside the ear line. Secure with a few stitches and cut the thread. Re-join the thread to the centre of the ear and work to the opposite edge in the same way. Turn under a tiny seam on the front edge of the ear and oversew this in position, working from the centre outwards each time. Repeat for the second ear.

PLACING THE NECK JOINT IN THE BODY

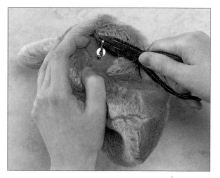

Each classic bear requires five crown joints. The four smallest are for the legs and arms and the largest, for the neck. The head is attached before the arms and legs.

1 Before the body is stuffed, the crown joints are fitted. Use a stiletto to ease aside the seam stitching gently at the centre top point of the body section. Insert the legs of the split pin through this hole and turn the top section of the body inside out.

2 Finish assembling the crown joint by threading on the second hardboard disc followed by a washer. Using sharp-nosed pliers, curl one pin over tightly, so that it sits against the washer and disc. Curl the second pin and check that the joint is firm.

STUFFING ARMS AND LEGS AND INSERTING CROWN JOINTS

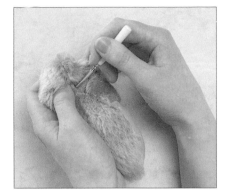

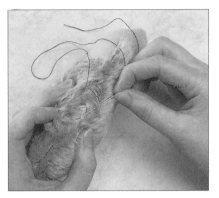

1 Stuff both arms and legs to within 2in (5cm) of the joint mark. From inside push a stiletto through this joint mark, carefully easing apart the threads of the fabric. Make a hole large enough for the split pin to fit. Assemble the remaining joints, threading on a washer and a disc. Push these through the holes in the arms and legs.

2 Finish stuffing each limb, packing the filling behind and around each hardboard disc until the required shape and firmness is achieved. Using matching sewing thread, ladder stitch the stuffing openings firmly closed on both arms and both legs, pushing in extra filling with the stuffing stick or a knitting needle as required while stitching.

3 Using a stiletto as before, make holes and insert the split pins at the points marked for placing both arms and legs on the bear's body. Thread on the second hardboard disc followed by a washer. Then complete the crown joints as described in Step 2 for the neck joints (see opposite page), making sure that each joint is firm.

STUFFING AND CLOSING THE BEAR'S BODY

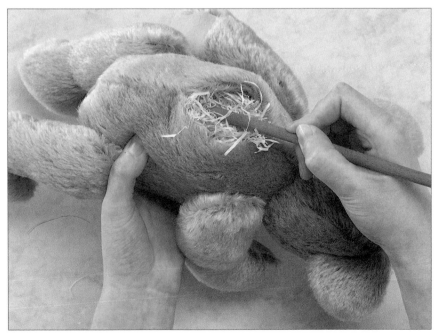

When all the joints are securely placed, stuff the body very firmly, pushing the stuffing down into position and shaping the bear as you work. (Before closing bear, see page 27 about growlers, squeakers, etc.) Ladder stitch the back opening of the bear closed, pulling the stitches firmly and fastening off securely.

The ladder stitching should not be visible on the surface of the bear.

TRIMMING THE BEAR'S MUZZLE

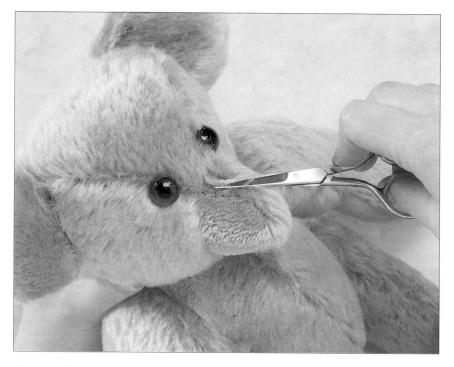

Great care should be taken when trimming any of the fur pile on your classic bear. Before beginning, test your trimming skills on a fur-fabric scrap or remnant.

If it is called for in the individual bear instructions, trim the pile around the muzzle. Use fine embroidery scissors and cut a little at a time until the required effect is achieved. For a traditional look, the muzzle should be trimmed all around to the point where the face begins to spread and flatten out. If in doubt, proceed very slowly and carefully, checking from time to time that the balance is correct.

EMBROIDERING THE BEAR'S FEATURES

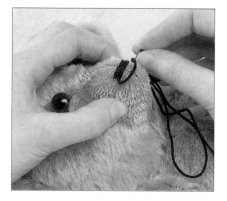

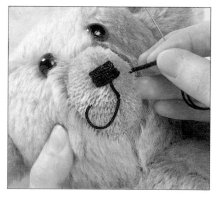

Worked in satin stitch, the bear's nose is usually made in a rectangular shape, but other shapes include hearts, triangles and ovals.

1 Embroidering features is the last stage in the bear-making process. With embroidery thread, embroider the nose in the desired shape, using closely worked satin stitches. It may be necessary to use pliers to pull the needle through when embroidering over seamlines.

2 Using straight stitches and embroidery thread, embroider the mouth. Experience will show the style of mouth you prefer, to create the right expression for your classic bear. If in doubt, unpick the mouth stitches and try again until you are completely satisfied with the result.

GROWLERS

For the ultimate touch of nostalgia a growler could be inserted in your bear before the stuffing opening on the body is closed. Growlers are best fitted in bears filled with wood wool, which, when tightly packed, will support their weight.

To insert a growler box, cut a circle of calico of sufficient size to enclose the growler completely. Place the growler, hole-end down in the centre of the calico fabric, pulling up the edges and gathering these over the opposite end. Wrap heavy-duty thread around the ends of the fabric a few times and tie off securely.

Half-fill the body of the bear with wood wool, packing it tightly into the lower section. Insert the growler so that the flat side is against the centre back of the body. Using a darning needle and heavy-duty thread, stitch the calico neatly to the fur fabric with tiny stitches that should be invisible on the right side. Finish off firmly. Continue to stuff the bear with wood wool, making sure this is tightly packed around the growler. Close the opening in the usual way with ladder stitching (see page 25).

SQUEAKERS

Bears fitted with squeakers should be soft enough to press and should not be laundered. A squeaker should be wrapped in calico and placed inside the bear in a similar manner to a growler (see instructions above), making sure that the reed is facing outwards.

TINKLERS

A tinkler, like a growler or a squeaker, must be inserted in a teddy bear before the stuffing opening on the bear's body is closed. It should be placed right in the middle of the bear. The bear should be large and well stuffed with wood wool.

MUSICAL BOXES

Before a musical box can be inserted in a bear, a calico cover should be made for it. The cover should have a hole through which the screw can be pushed. The calico is then stitched to the back of the bear in a similar manner to a growler, with the screw facing the fur fabric. A stiletto can then be used to make a hole through which to push the screw before the key is replaced. As with other 'voices', the bear should be firmly stuffed with wood wool which will hold the movement rigidly in position.

When making collectors' bears always use the best quality bear fittings.

Below are shown (from left to right and interspersed with sewing equipment) wood wool, eyes, hardboard crown joints, a teasel brush, plastic squeakers, a growler box and a musical box.

BEAR CARE AND REPAIR

Both new and old classic bears should be looked after carefully in order to preserve them in the best possible condition. The high acid content of straw and wood wool stuffing can cause bears to rot and the natural fibres used in their textiles can dry with age, making them prone to tear at the slightest pressure.

Strong sunlight or artificial light that contains ultra-violet rays can also prove damaging, so always keep bears away from prolonged exposure.

Before attempting to use a vacuum cleaner to remove dust from a classic bear, cover the hose nozzle with a piece of net or gauze

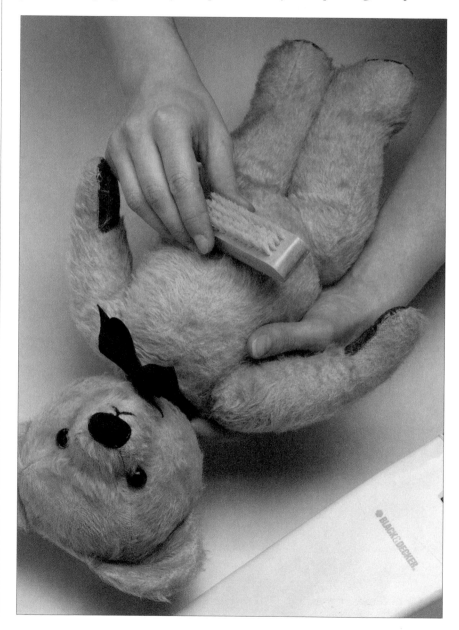

Read the instructions for cleaning classic bears on the opposite page before brushing a valuable bear.

For a permanent display of bears it is best to use a tungsten light bulb. Fluctuations in temperature should also be avoided, so do remember to keep bears away from any source of heat, such as a radiator, convector heater or even hot water pipes.

Collectors' bears should always be handled with clean hands and in the case of valuable bears, it is wise to wear cotton gloves. The grime and acid on the hands can inflict untold damage on delicate fabrics.

Remember that collectors' bears and the bears in this book should not be given to small children to play with, as they do not comply with toy safety regulations.

CLEANING CLASSIC BEARS

Dust can also prove a problem. It too has a high acid content and bears on display should be vacuumed regularly to remove any particles that may have settled. To minimise the risk of damaging the bear, cover the hose nozzle of the vacuum cleaner with a piece of fine net or gauze, which can be held in place with an elastic band. Then run the nozzle gently over the bear, taking extra care around the eyes, over the embroidered areas and along the seams – all places where dust is most likely to settle.

It is possible to freshen the fur pile of a bear by scrubbing it gently with a soft tooth brush or natural bristle nail brush which has been dipped in a very weak solution of detergent. The liquid type used for washing delicate clothes is best. Great care must be taken not to let the water soak into the backing fabric, as this might be absorbed into the wood wool filling. The fur can then be wiped gently with a clean damp cloth until both the detergent and grime have been removed. It cannot, however, be stressed strongly enough that you should not attempt to wash a valuable bear without seeking advice from an expert such as the curator of a museum specializing in childhood toys and memorabilia. Specialist companies are now developing dry-cleaning fluids for bears and the manufacturers' instructions should always be followed carefully.

REPAIRING BEARS

Restorers who specialize in making good the wear and tear inflicted by the years can also be found. Unless you are very sure of what you are doing, or the bear is of little value, do not attempt do-it-yourself repairs.

Obviously, seams can be restitched using a good quality thread and a ladder-stitch technique and eyes can be replaced using reproduction glass boot buttons or modern amber ones. However, never make a repair or alteration that cannot be easily removed, thus restoring the bear to its original condition. This is particularly true of replacement paw and foot pads.

STORING BEARS

A well-loved collectors' bear that is beginning to show its age should be wrapped in acid-free tissue paper and stored in a sturdy cardboard box. On no account should it be wrapped in polythene or plastic. It is possible that an old bear may have had its stuffing eaten by mites, in which case the seams should be opened gently, and the remaining stuffing removed. The bear should then be treated with a suitable proprietary insect repellant before being restuffed with wood wool and its seams restitched. Again, if in any doubt, it is always wise to consult an expert before attempting any repairs.

Take good care of your traditionally made teddy bears and they will be a joy for collectors in the future.

EARLY BLACK BEAR

The bear pictured here was inspired by early black bears. Made from black bouclé woven fabric, it is 16in (41cm) tall and has a black velvet muzzle and pads.

Some years before the official birth of the teddy bear in 1903, both stuffed and wooden bears were being sold as toys. Unlike the teddies of later years, these bears were made to sound fierce and lifelike with a sinister growl; hardly the cuddly confidante of childhood!

These forerunners of the modern teddy were based on the bears of the wild. Known as 'bruins', they stood on all fours and usually had a humped back. Often they were made from real fur; they had snarling expressions and some even had clockwork mechanisms to open their mouths in a realistic growl.

Some of these lifelike bears were muzzled and chained, resembling the dancing bears of middle European countries of the time. These poor bears stared through sad eyes over the straps and harnesses used to fetter them.

By today's more enlightened standards, we look at these early examples of bears as being pathetic and miserable! They certainly were not made to be cuddled and loved.

Russian children of the time were no strangers to bears in captivity. One particular bear – Mishka – is traditional to Russian folklore and is looked upon as part of the national heritage. (More recently he appeared as the national emblem for the Moscow Olympic games held in 1980). Certainly, carved wooden bears that could perform simple tricks were produced in Russia, alongside somersaulting bears and bears that could walk across the floor. Once again, these were amusing pieces, but far removed from the teddy bear.

There was also a range of German-produced bears known as Peter bears. With their rolling eyes, moving tongues and bared teeth, they would probably have startled most adults, let alone a small child! Examples of these ferocious animals still exist; and although they post-date early teddy bear manufacture by a couple of decades (historians put their production around 1925), they are more advanced and more frightening versions of the original bruins.

Although we tend to think of teddy bears in golden plush fur

fabric, many early bears were black or dark brown. In the dawn of teddy bear production, black and dark brown bears were still popular, particularly with German manufacturers. Unlike their predecessors, these are proper teddies with all the charm of their breed. The bear featured here is reminiscent of a Steiff bear produced in 1912 which, in fact, had beige felt pads and glowing, red tinted eyes (they were shiny black buttons on circles of orange felt). The ferocious Victorian bruins would, almost without exception, have had black glass eyes and dark paw and foot pads.

Early bears were intended to issue a fierce growl, although often it sounded more as though they were mooing! Although this bear has a friendly disposition, a growling voicebox would add to its authenticity and old-fashioned appeal.

A growler can be inserted quite easily – instructions on how to do this appear on page 27.

Materials

½yd (45cm) of 54in (137cm) wide black bouclé woven fabric with man–made pile
9in (23cm) square of black velvet
Tacking (basting) thread
Matching sewing thread
Matching heavy-duty thread
One 2½in (64mm) hardboard crown joint
Four 2in (50mm) hardboard crown joints
Small amount of 'firm-fill' polyester filling (stuffing)
1½ lb (680g) wood wool
Two ⅝in (17mm) black boot button eyes
One skein black 'pearl cotton' embroidery thread

MAKING THE EARLY BLACK BEAR

Before starting to make the bear, carefully read the chapter on Classic Bear-making. Following the step-by-step instructions there, make the 10 templates, cut out the fabric pieces and assemble the bear, taking into consideration the special points below. Take care to keep your working surfaces as clean as possible at all times.

This bouclé fabric is not easy to sew and beginners are advised to practice on the more usual fur pile fabrics before attempting a bear of this type. The backing fabric is quite stiff and it may be necessary to use a pair of pliers and a stronger needle (such as a darner) when hand stitching or tacking (basting). The pile is not so easily trapped in the seams, but these should be checked and any caught threads teased out using a bodkin or stiletto. Do not use a teasel brush on bouclé fabrics.

The muzzle of this bear is cut out separately in velvet. Before sewing the head gusset to the side-of-head pieces following the step-by-step instructions, join the two velvet side-muzzle pieces to the two side-of-head pieces (seams B-C). Then join the velvet top muzzle to the head gusset (seam B-B).

As velvet tends to 'slip' as it is machine sewn, it is advisable to hand stitch paw and foot pads, using a doubled thread and a firm backstitch. Tack (baste) both paw and foot pads in position as shown in the step-by-step instructions on page 21 for foot pads, using smaller and closer stitches than normal.

The eyes are placed on the head gusset seam, so that their lower edges are 1in (2.5cm) from the start of the velvet muzzle.

The ears should be set towards the back of the head across the gusset seams and at a slight angle with the lower edges tilting forwards a little.

The nose is worked in horizontal satin stitches across the seam at the end of the muzzle, forming a rectangle about ¾in (2cm) wide and ¼in (7mm) deep. Using two strands of pearl cotton, work a ½in (12mm) straight stitch downwards from the nose along the lower muzzle seam. Then work a ⅝in (18mm) straight stitch to either side to form the mouth.

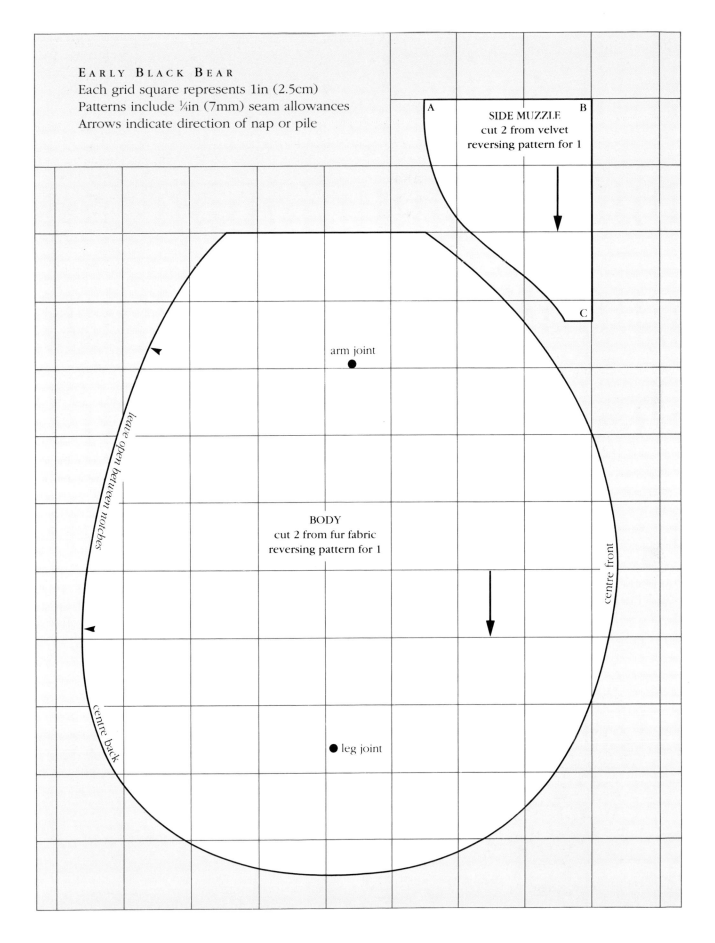

EARLY BLACK BEAR
Each grid square represents 1in (2.5cm)
Patterns include ¼in (7mm) seam allowances
Arrows indicate direction of nap or pile

A   B
SIDE MUZZLE
cut 2 from velvet
reversing pattern for 1

C

arm joint

leave open between notches

BODY
cut 2 from fur fabric
reversing pattern for 1

centre front

centre back

leg joint

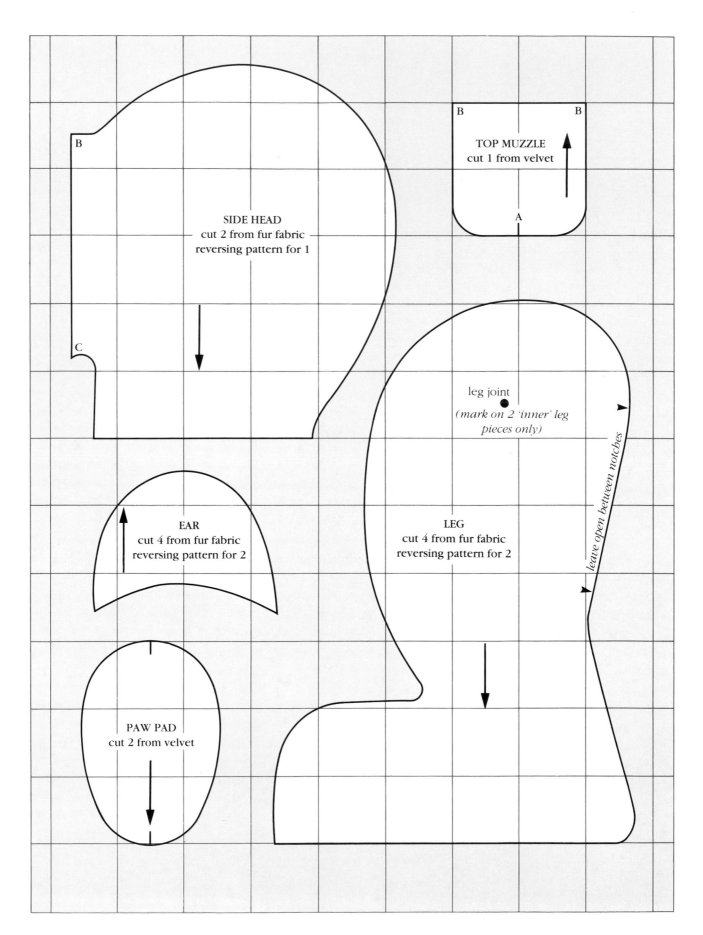

SIDE HEAD
cut 2 from fur fabric
reversing pattern for 1

B

C

TOP MUZZLE
cut 1 from velvet

B   B

A

leg joint
(mark on 2 'inner' leg
pieces only)

LEG
cut 4 from fur fabric
reversing pattern for 2

leave open between notches

EAR
cut 4 from fur fabric
reversing pattern for 2

PAW PAD
cut 2 from velvet

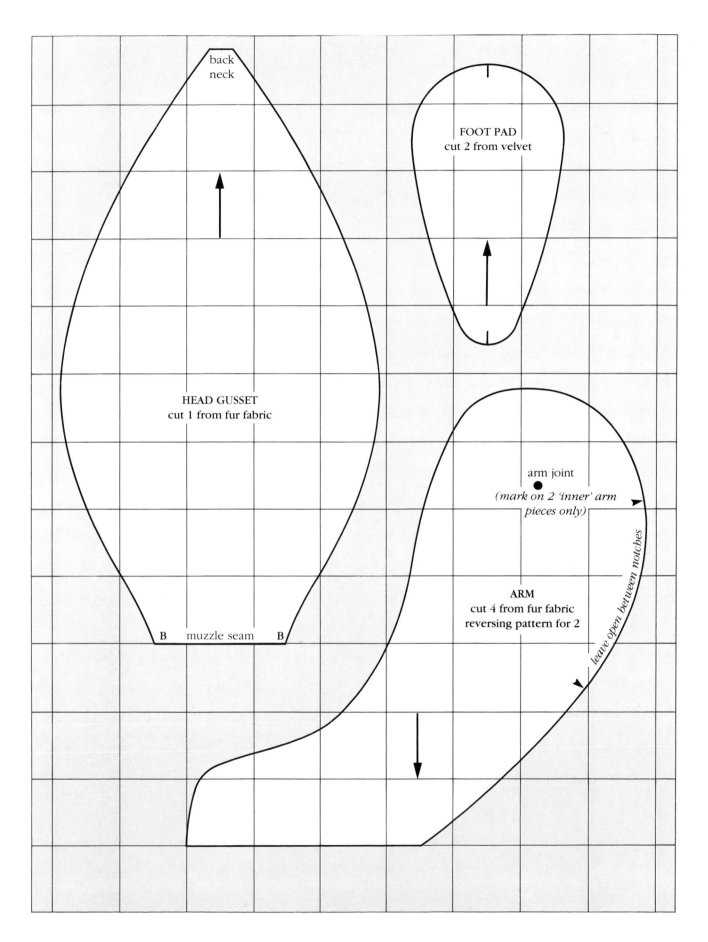

back
neck

FOOT PAD
cut 2 from velvet

HEAD GUSSET
cut 1 from fur fabric

arm joint
*(mark on 2 'inner' arm
pieces only)*

ARM
cut 4 from fur fabric
reversing pattern for 2

leave open between notches

B   muzzle seam   B

MICHTOM BEAR

The bear pictured here was inspired by Michtom bears. Made from honey-gold mohair pile fabric, it is 18in (46cm) tall and it has mushroom-coloured suedette paw and foot pads.

The creation of a jointed, mohair pile bear, was the inspiration of a Russian immigrant to the United States named Morris Michtom.

Michtom ran a small candy store in Brooklyn with his wife, Rose, a skilled toymaker and seamstress. Many of her toys adorned the shop window to encourage customers inside.

The enterprising Mr Michtom seized upon the idea of the toy bear while reading the *Washington Evening Post* one November day in 1902. A political cartoon, showing President Theodore Roosevelt refusing to shoot a tethered bear cub, gave Michtom the idea for an endearing toy bear. Michtom persuaded his wife to make a prototype cuddly bear. It was to be the first of many.

The original Michtom bear was made from golden plush mohair. It stood 21in (53cm) tall, with long, rather thin, arms and legs which had pale felt paws embroidered with black, straight-stitched claws. The bear's large, rounded ears were set on the sides of its head and it viewed the world from small, black, boot button eyes. The rather pensive and woebegone expression of Rose Michtom's toy bear proved an instant success.

The shrewd Mr Michtom, so the story goes, sent a presentation bear to the White House asking for permission to name it in honour of the President. 'I don't believe that my name will do much for the image of your stuffed bear,' President Roosevelt allegedly replied, 'but you have my permission to use it'.

Whether Teddy Roosevelt's name did, in fact, do much, or whether the lovable little bear with its big round ears simply caught the imagination of the public does not really matter. 'Teddy's bear' was taken into the hearts and homes of many American families.

The Michtom bear was soon being distributed through wholesalers Butler Brothers and from these simple beginnings the hugely successful Ideal Novelty and Toy Company was formed in Brooklyn.

In fact, so successful was the Michtom's teddy, that many imitators jumped on the bear bandwagon, producing teddy bear lookalikes.

Certainly, by 1907, teddy bears had taken America by storm. Although teddy bear history is poorly documented, evidence of

these creatures' popularity was immortalized in the much-loved music, *Teddy Bears' Picnic*, composed in this year by W J Bratton. The lyrics to the piece were added later.

One of the original Michtom bears now resides at the Smithsonian Institute in Washington, DC, but you can make your own version displaying some of its charming characteristics by using the following pattern instructions.

The Michtom bear, in common with most bears in this book, can be stuffed with either a polyester or wood wool filling (stuffing). The latter creates a lot of dust, so asthma sufferers would be advised to wear a mask when using it.

Materials

½yd (45cm) of 54in (137cm) wide honey-gold mohair with ⅜in (9mm) pile

Small square of mushroom-coloured suedette

Tacking (basting) thread

Matching sewing thread

Matching heavy-duty thread

One 2in (50mm) hardboard crown joint

Four 1⅜in (36mm) hardboard crown joints

Small amount of 'firm-fill' polyester filling (stuffing)

1½lb (680g) wood wool

Two ½in (14mm) black buttons for eyes

One skein black 'stranded cotton' embroidery thread

MAKING THE MICHTOM BEAR

Before starting to make the bear, carefully read the chapter on Classic Bear-making. Following the step-by-step instructions there, make the 10 templates, cut out the fabric pieces and assemble the bear, taking into consideration the special points below. Take care to keep your working surfaces as clean as possible at all times.

When using wood wool, always stuff the point of the muzzle, the feet and front paws with polyester filling (stuffing) first. This will ensure a smooth and even shape. Additional wood wool can be added to give extra firmness, but the smoother polyester should always remain as a protective layer beneath the fabric.

After stuffing and before finally closing the back opening, use polyester filler to pad out the hump and back curve fully.

If you wish to use black buttons for the eyes, it may be necessary to enlarge the stiletto hole by carefully cutting a few strands of ground fabric to enable the shank of the button to slip through. The eyes should be set just below the head gusset seam lines, level with the lower edge of the ears.

The claws are formed by embroidering three straight stitches on each foot pad and four straight stitches on each paw pad, using six strands of black stranded cotton embroidery thread.

The ears should be positioned from the head gusset seam downwards following the stitching line of the lower dart.

The nose is worked in horizontal satin stitches across the seam at the end of the muzzle, forming a rectangle about ⅝in (16mm) wide and ½in (12mm) deep. Using 6 strands of stranded cotton, work a ¼in (7cm) straight stitch downwards from the nose along the lower muzzle seam; then work a ½in (12mm) straight stitch to either side to form the mouth.

Finally, trim the fur pile back close around the whole of the muzzle. The pile around the teddy bear's eyes should also be trimmed lightly to expose them fully.

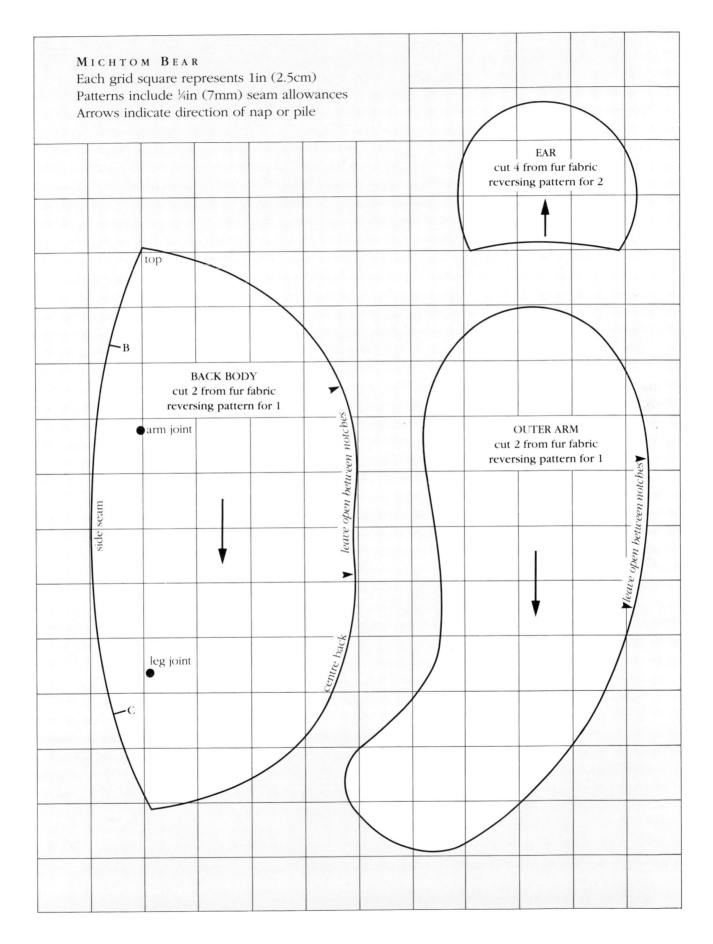

MICHTOM BEAR
Each grid square represents 1in (2.5cm)
Patterns include ¼in (7mm) seam allowances
Arrows indicate direction of nap or pile

EAR
cut 4 from fur fabric
reversing pattern for 2

BACK BODY
cut 2 from fur fabric
reversing pattern for 1

top

B

arm joint

side seam

leg joint

C

leave open between notches

centre back

OUTER ARM
cut 2 from fur fabric
reversing pattern for 1

leave open between notches

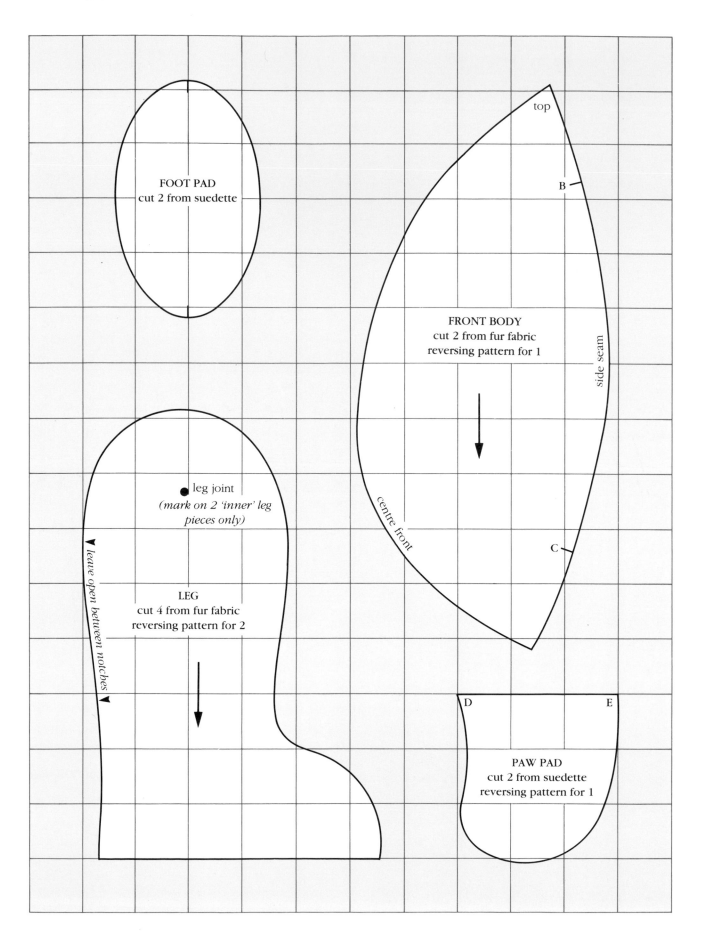

FOOT PAD
cut 2 from suedette

top

B

FRONT BODY
cut 2 from fur fabric
reversing pattern for 1

side seam

centre front

C

● leg joint
*(mark on 2 'inner' leg
pieces only)*

◄ *leave open between notches*
◄

LEG
cut 4 from fur fabric
reversing pattern for 2

D   E

PAW PAD
cut 2 from suedette
reversing pattern for 1

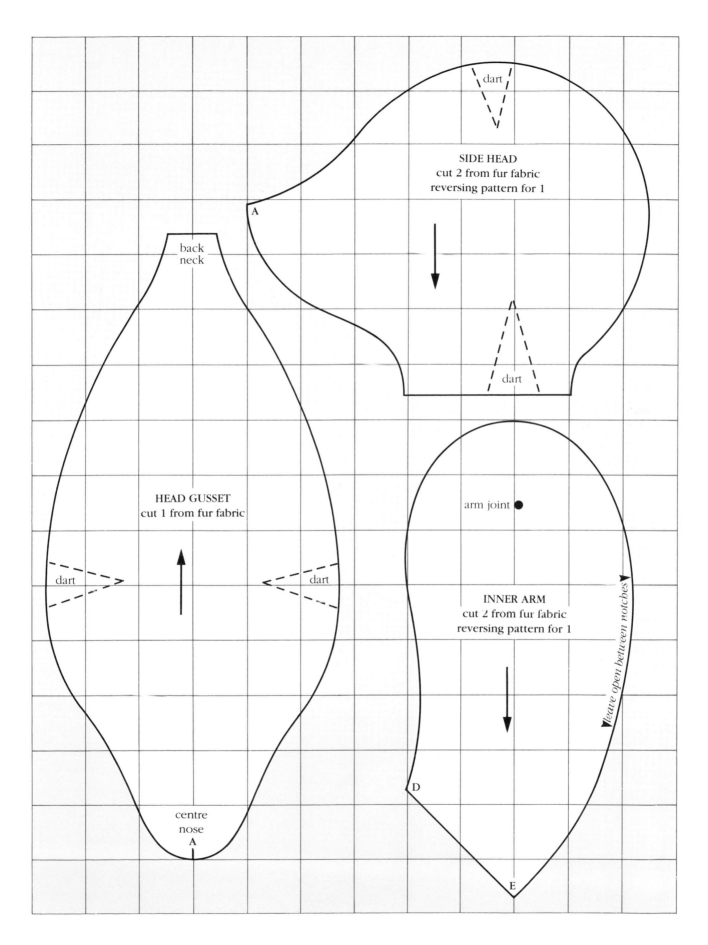

dart

SIDE HEAD
cut 2 from fur fabric
reversing pattern for 1

dart

A

back
neck

arm joint ●

HEAD GUSSET
cut 1 from fur fabric

dart   dart

INNER ARM
cut 2 from fur fabric
reversing pattern for 1

leave open between notches

centre
nose
A

D

E

EARLY GERMAN BEAR

The bear pictured here was inspired by early German bears. Made from honey-beige distressed pile mohair fabric, it is 14½in (37cm) tall and has pale beige suedette paw and foot pads.

Although disabled from childhood by polio, German-born Margarete Steiff conquered her disability to become a world-renowned toy maker. And it is for the Steiff teddy bears that she is probably best known. Without doubt, the toy bears created by the Steiff factory in the early part of this century are the great-grandfathers of today's teddies.

History is still slightly confused over the origins of the Steiff bear, although it is commonly thought the toy was the brainchild of Margarete's nephew, Richard, who often sketched bears at Stuttgart Zoo.

It evidently took several years to persuade Margarete Steiff that bears with movable joints and plush fur were the toy of the future, but after setbacks and various modifications, the first Steiff bear – called Friend Petz – was completed in time for the Leipzig Toy Fair of 1903. Even then, it looked as though the bear was destined for the reject pile, as no one showed any particular interest. On the last day of the Fair, a leading New York toy importer approached the Steiff stand. It is said he was disappointed that there were no really new or exciting toys that year. Friend Petz was brought to his attention by Richard and so enthralled him that he placed an order for 3,000 bears there and then. The Steiff legend was born!

Over the few years following the Leipzig Toy Fair, bear production rose rapidly. By 1907 an amazing 974,000 bears were produced. Steiff led the bear market! Even today, this is remembered as the year of the bear.

Around 1914 the Steiff style began to change; the hump disappeared and the muzzle shortened and thickened. Bears in general took on a friendlier form. From 1920, the stuffing changed from wood wool to kapok and by 1921, glass eyes replaced boot buttons.

Classic Steiff bears can now be expected to fetch sums in excess of four figures when sold at auction today. All bears manufactured by the company before 1910 are extremely valuable and the few with their growlers still working prove particularly desirable.

The record price for a bear at auction is held by the 1920s Steiff bear, 'Happy', made in dual plush fabric. Originally purchased in Ireland, it had been with the same family for some time. It was bought for a staggering £55,000 ($81,000) by the chairman of a modern teddy bear manufacturer on behalf of a

*The Steiff button label above
is dated circa 1910.*

Materials

*½yd (45cm) of 54in (137cm)
  wide honey-beige distressed
  pile mohair with ½in
  (12mm) pile
Small square of pale beige
  suedette
Tacking (basting) thread
Matching sewing thread
Matching heavy-duty thread
One 1⅜in (35mm)
  hardboard crown joint
Four 1in (25mm) hardboard
  crown joints
Small amount of 'firm-fill'
  polyester filling (stuffing)
1lb (450 g) wood wool
Two ⅝in (16mm) amber and
  black glass boot button eyes
One skein black 'soft cotton'
  and one skein terracotta
  'stranded cotton'
  embroidery thread*

friend. (By the time you read this, this record price for a teddy bear at auction might easily have been surpassed.)

It was as early as 1905 that the firm of Steiff protected its products by registering its now famous 'button in the ear' trademark. Although other companies tried to imitate this, legal action prevented them from doing so.

This delightful bear has some of the characteristics of a Steiff creation of around 1904. It has a marked hump and long, slim, curved arms with claws embroidered in terracotta thread on its paw pads. Its nose is worked in satin stitch onto a thin, tapering muzzle and its rounded ears are set vertically across the head gusset seams. Instead of wooden boot buttons, it has amber glass eyes, set rather close together, and it is made in long pile distressed honey-beige mohair to provide a classic effect.

MAKING THE EARLY GERMAN BEAR

Before starting to make the bear, carefully read the chapter on Classic Bear-making. Following the step-by-step instructions there, make the 9 templates, cut out the fabric pieces and assemble the bear, taking into consideration the special points below. Take care to keep your working surfaces as clean as possible at all times.

Unlike other bears in this book, those made from distressed pile mohair should not be brushed with a teasel brush, as this is likely to alter the characteristics of the fabric.

The claws are formed by embroidering four straight stitches on each of the bear's two paw pads, using six strands of terracotta stranded cotton embroidery thread.

The eyes are placed just below the head gusset seam, so that their lower edges are 2in (5cm) from the tip of the muzzle.

The muzzle is trimmed back slightly unevenly, and a small amount of pile is cut away around the eyes to improve their appearance.

The ears should be set at the top of the head across the gusset seams and about 1½in (4cm) apart.

The nose is worked in horizontal satin stitches across the tip of the muzzle, using black soft cotton embroidery thread and forming a triangle. Using two strands of black soft cotton embroidery thread, work a ¼in (7mm) straight stitch downwards from the tip of the nose along the lower muzzle seam. Then using a single strand of the same thread, work a ½in (12mm) straight stitch upwards to either side to form the smiling mouth.

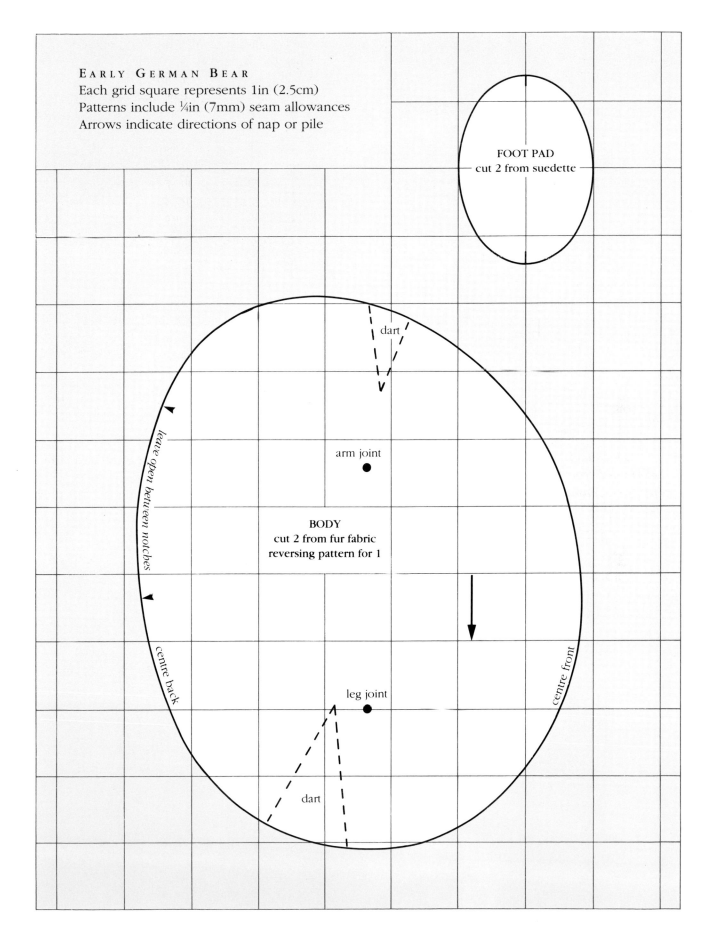

EARLY GERMAN BEAR
Each grid square represents 1in (2.5cm)
Patterns include ¼in (7mm) seam allowances
Arrows indicate directions of nap or pile

FOOT PAD
cut 2 from suedette

dart

leave open between notches

arm joint

BODY
cut 2 from fur fabric
reversing pattern for 1

centre back

centre front

leg joint

dart

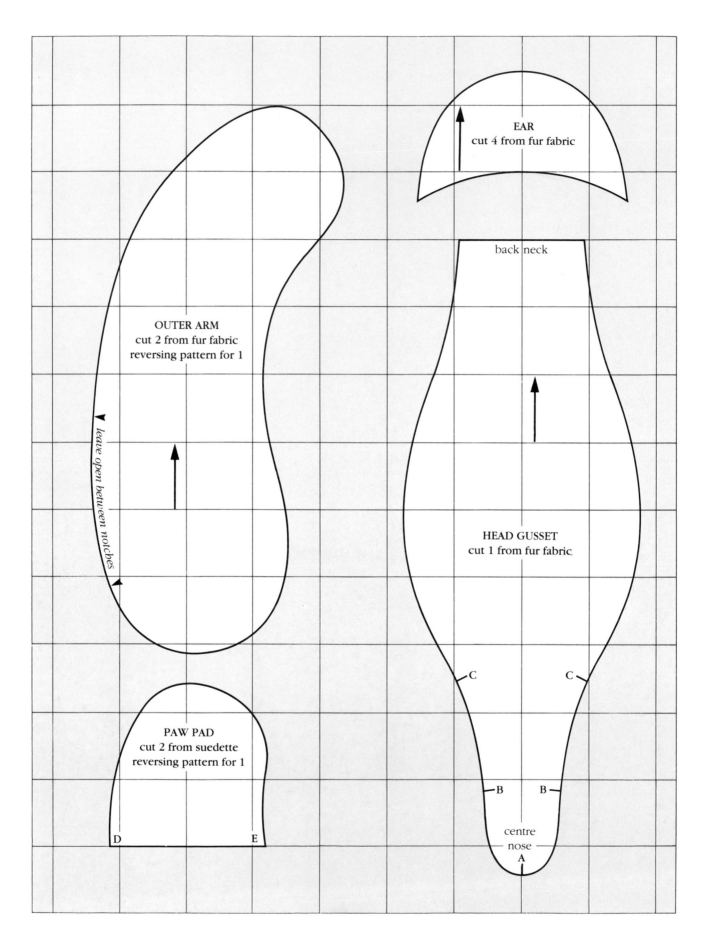

EAR
cut 4 from fur fabric

back neck

OUTER ARM
cut 2 from fur fabric
reversing pattern for 1

leave open between notches

HEAD GUSSET
cut 1 from fur fabric

C   C

PAW PAD
cut 2 from suedette
reversing pattern for 1

D   E

B   B

centre
nose
A

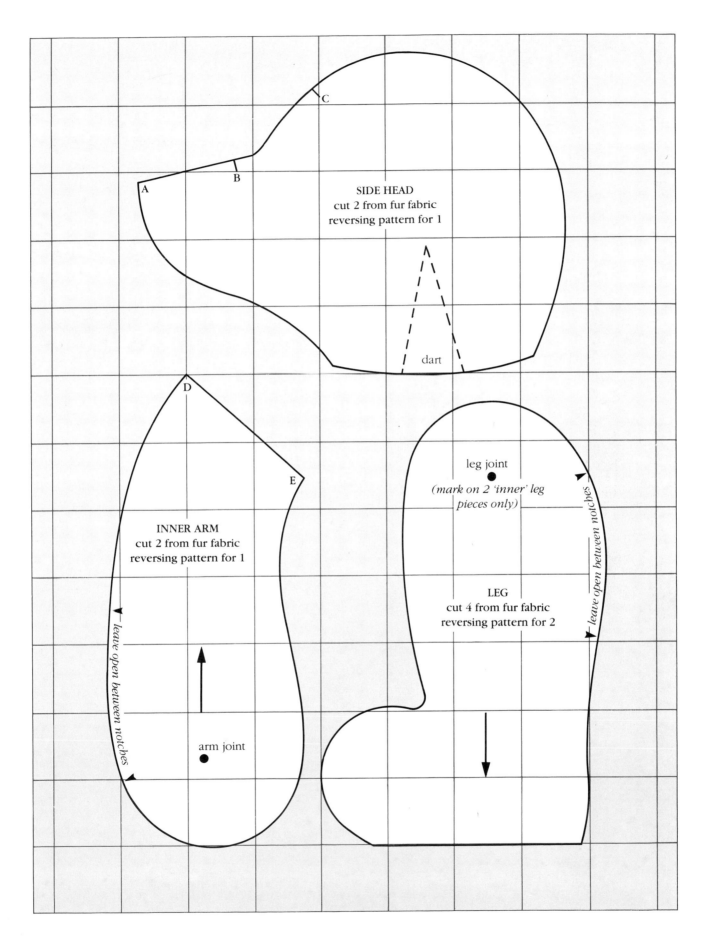

C

B

A

SIDE HEAD
cut 2 from fur fabric
reversing pattern for 1

dart

D

E

INNER ARM
cut 2 from fur fabric
reversing pattern for 1

leave open between notches

arm joint ●

leg joint
●
*(mark on 2 'inner' leg
pieces only)*

leave open between notches

LEG
cut 4 from fur fabric
reversing pattern for 2

1920s GERMAN BEAR

The bear pictured here was inspired by 1920s German bears. Made from gold crushed pile mohair fabric, it is 18in (46cm) tall and has light beige suedette pads.

Up until the outbreak of World War I in 1914, the basic teddy bear had changed little from its early beginnings. However, the war brought disruption to trading and production, and it wasn't until the turn of the decade that bears again began to fill the shelves.

By the 1920s, German bears were once more exported in large numbers. Factories such as Bing, Gebrüder Hermann, Gebrüder Sussenguth and, of course, Steiff, were all in evidence.

Bing bears, as they came to be known, were mechanical and often colourfully dressed. Gebrüder Sussenguth produced the rather ferocious Peter bears already discussed on page 30. Hermann bears, on the other hand, closely resembled the famous Steiff bears. In fact, the Hermann company was founded in 1907 specifically to make bears. It was only in later years that the company widened its range to include other toys.

However, by the 1920s, the German manufacturers were up against stiff competition from a growing number of toy companies in other countries manufacturing teddy bears for the first time.

In Britain, Chad Valley had made use of the war, which blocked German imports, to firmly establish itself as a soft toy manufacturer. Its teddy bears did not roll off the production line though till 1920.

Like Steiff bears, the Chad Valley ones bore a metal trade button quite often clipped to the ear.

Other major manufacturers included Dean's and J K Farnell in Britain and the Ideal Toy Company and Knickerbocker Toy Company in America.

By the 1920s, bears were evolving into a more modern design. Glass eyes were replacing boot buttons, the hump was beginning to lessen in size, the limbs began to shorten and the torso grew more rotund. In other words, the bears became more cuddly than they had been before. The stuffing for bears had also changed as they evolved.

Many bears manufactured in the 1920s were stuffed with a substance known as 'Aerolite'. This was the trade name for kapok, a natural fibre which can be mixed with wood wool or sawdust (and indeed it was) to create a softer feel.

One of the most famous bears from the early 1920s is surely Winnie-the-Pooh, a character created by A A Milne and almost certainly inspired by

This German bear (1910-20) is only 8in (20cm) tall.

Materials

½yd (45cm) of 54in (137cm) wide gold crushed pile mohair (with ¾in (21mm) pile

Small square of tight beige suedette

Tacking (basting) thread

Matching sewing thread

Matching heavy-duty thread

One 3in (76mm) hardboard crown joint

Four 2in (50mm) hardboard crown joints

2lb (1kg) 'firm-fill' polyester filling (stuffing)

Two ⅝in (17mm) black glass boot button eyes

One skein black 'pearl cotton' embroidery thread

a J K Farnell bear. However, the illustrations of Pooh, drawn by Ernest Shepard, are modelled upon a Steiff bear called Growler.

The other notable bear of the period is 'Happy', a brown-tipped, beige, dual plush mohair bear from the Steiff factory. Happy was sold at auction in 1989 for a record sum of £55,000 ($81,000), making it the most expensive teddy bear in the world to date.

The bear featured here has large, narrow feet in the classic style and large round ears set wide apart. It has long, slim arms and light beige suedette foot and paw pads. Although toy bears were evolving at this time, German manufacturers, more than others, continued to make the traditional long-muzzled bears.

This bear has black glass boot button eyes and a black embroidered nose, but brown glass eyes and a brown embroidered nose and mouth could be substituted to achieve a closer resemblance to Happy. The famous bear's pads were made from a yellowish, beige felt; velveteen or suedette would make an acceptable substitute.

MAKING THE 1920s GERMAN BEAR

Before starting to make the bear, carefully read the chapter on Classic Bear-making. Following the step-by-step instructions there, make the 9 templates, cut out the fabric pieces and assemble the bear, taking into consideration the special points below. Take care to keep your working surfaces as clean as possible at all times.

When working with extra long pile mohair, great care must be taken at the cutting stage. Use small, pointed and very sharp scissors, ensuring that only the backing fabric is cut. As each piece is finished, pull it away from the fabric carefully, separating the mohair strands as you do so.

As the pattern pieces are pinned and then tacked (basted) together, try using the flat of the pin or needle to push the pile inwards. This will help when the seams are machine stitched, preventing excessive amounts of pile being caught in the stitches.

The muzzle of this bear is left untrimmed. However, it may be advisable to trim away the pile in the area of the nose, before stitching. This will give a much neater effect and make working easier. Some pile may be trimmed from around the eyes if preferred.

The eyes are placed on the head gusset seam, so that their lower edges are 2½in (6.5cm) from the centre of the tip of the nose.

The ears should be set about 2in (5cm) apart across the gusset seams and at a slight angle with the lower edges tilting forwards a little.

The nose is worked in vertical satin stitches across the seam at the end of the muzzle, forming a rectangle about ¾in (2cm) wide and ½in (12mm) deep. The bear has no embroidered mouth.

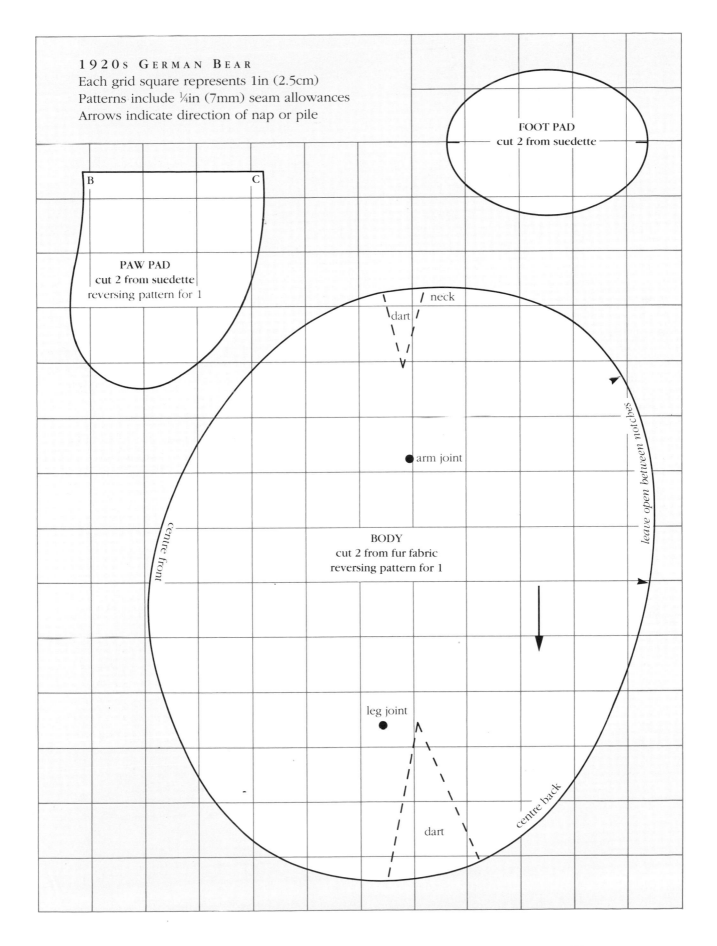

1920s GERMAN BEAR
Each grid square represents 1in (2.5cm)
Patterns include ¼in (7mm) seam allowances
Arrows indicate direction of nap or pile

FOOT PAD
cut 2 from suedette

B   C

PAW PAD
cut 2 from suedette
reversing pattern for 1

neck

dart

arm joint

centre front

leave open between notches

BODY
cut 2 from fur fabric
reversing pattern for 1

leg joint

centre back

dart

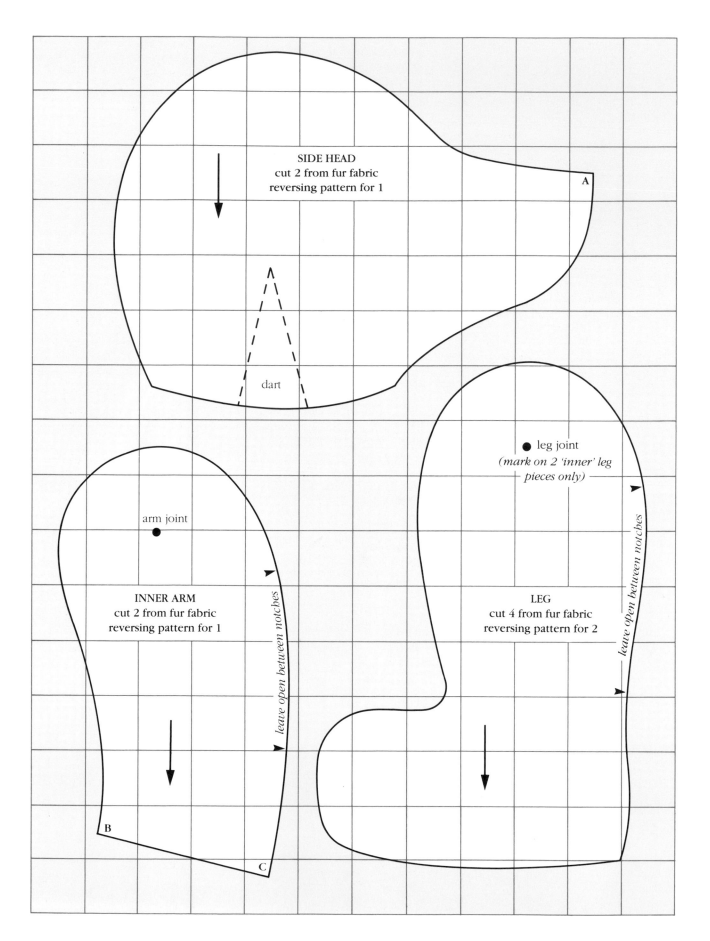

SIDE HEAD
cut 2 from fur fabric
reversing pattern for 1

A

dart

● leg joint
(*mark on 2 'inner' leg
pieces only*)

arm joint

INNER ARM
cut 2 from fur fabric
reversing pattern for 1

LEG
cut 4 from fur fabric
reversing pattern for 2

leave open between notches

leave open between notches

B

C

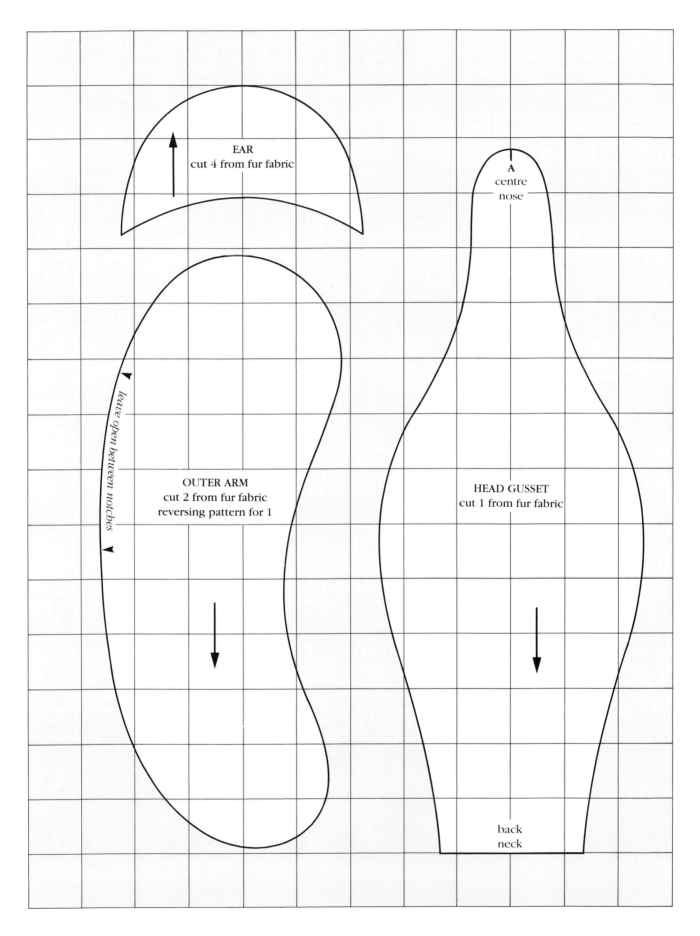

EAR
cut 4 from fur fabric

A
centre
nose

leave open between notches

OUTER ARM
cut 2 from fur fabric
reversing pattern for 1

HEAD GUSSET
cut 1 from fur fabric

back
neck

MINIATURE BEAR

The bear pictured here was inspired by miniature classic bears. Made from honeysuckle mohair pile fabric, it is 7in (18cm) tall and has cream felt foot pads.

Once teddy bears had established themselves firmly in the toy trade, so various manifestations appeared. One of the most endearing and popular types was the tiny or miniature bear.

What defines a real miniature is often subject to conjecture. One of the early Steiff lines was a small bear of 9in (23cm) in height, but it is generally agreed that bears must be no taller than 7in (18cm) to be classed as miniature.

One of the principal manufacturers of tiny bears was Schreyer, a German company, often known more commonly as Schuco. Established in 1912, the company produced an unusual range of bears over the years. Its tiny stuffed bears were often made in various colours; the smallest one measured just over 2in (5cm) tall. Schuco also manufactured bears which could nod or shake their heads. These 'Yes/No' teddy bears were also produced in miniature versions.

During the 1920s scent bottles and lipstick cases came in the guise of little bears to put into a handbag or evening purse.

Miniature bears have the advantage that they can be popped into a pocket and carried around with their owner. Many people profess to having a miniature bear mascot which accompanies them everywhere. Small bears require a great deal of skill and patience to produce. Seams must be very accurately sewn and care must be taken when turning tiny sections, such as arms and legs. However, there is great satisfaction and pleasure in the final results, which have a distinctive charm. The obvious choice of fabric would be a short-piled mohair, but camel hair, cashmere or mohair cloth would be equally acceptable.

The bear featured here is jointed with the smallest commercially produced hardboard joints, but the joints for smaller bears can be made from two buttons, which can be pulled together using heavy duty thread. However, these joints will not be so readily moveable as a crown joint. Do take care when bending the split pin on some small joints, as they can be particularly unyielding. In some cases it may be best to substitute a longer pin, which can be curved over several times.

Some classic miniature bears were filled with sawdust, as wood wool would prove almost impossible to use.

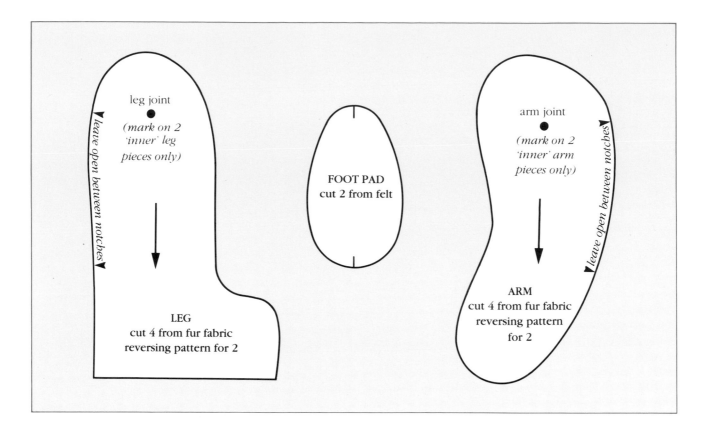

leg joint

●

(mark on 2
'inner' leg
pieces only)

leave open between notches

LEG
cut 4 from fur fabric
reversing pattern
for 2

FOOT PAD
cut 2 from felt

arm joint

●

(mark on 2
'inner' arm
pieces only)

leave open between notches

ARM
cut 4 from fur fabric
reversing pattern
for 2

Materials

*¼yd (25cm) of 54in (137cm)
wide honeysuckle mohair
with ⅜in (9mm) pile (this
will be enough for several
bears)*

*3in (7.5cm) square of cream-
coloured felt*

Tacking (basting) thread

Matching sewing thread

Matching heavy-duty thread

Black heavy-duty thread

*One 1in (25mm) hardboard
crown joint*

*Four ¾in (18mm) hardboard
crown joints*

*4oz (110 g) 'firm-fill'
polyester filling (stuffing)*

*Two small round black glass
beads*

*One skein black 'stranded
cotton' embroidery thread*

MAKING THE MINIATURE BEAR

Before starting to make the bear, carefully read the chapter on Classic Bear-making. Following the step-by-step instructions there, make the 7 templates, cut out the fabric pieces and assemble the bear, taking into consideration the special points below.

Great care must be taken when machine stitching such a small bear. Seam allowances should be kept to a minimum – about ³⁄₁₆in (5mm). Areas which need special attention such as the pads and the muzzle are best stitched by hand, using a doubled thread and a firm backstitch. Any points which are likely to be strained during stuffing should be hand stitched with a double row of stitches.

The position of the eyes will depend on the size and shape of the beads chosen. This bear has eyes placed just outside the head gusset about ¾in (18mm) from the tip of the nose. Bead eyes are applied using a similar technique to glass, except that they sit on the fur fabric and are not inserted through it. Heavy-duty black thread should be used. This should be taken from the position of the ear, through the head, to the point where the bead is to sit. Thread on the bead and settle it against the head, checking that the position is correct. Take a small stitch the width of the bead back into the head and take the needle across to the position of the second eye. Fasten this with another straight stitch and take the needle to the second ear position before finishing off.

The nose is worked in horizontal satin stitches using six strands of black stranded cotton and forming a small rectangle. From the centre of the nose a ¼in (7mm) straight stitch is taken down the seamline and a smiling mouth is then made by taking a straight stitch to left and right upwards and outwards to each side.

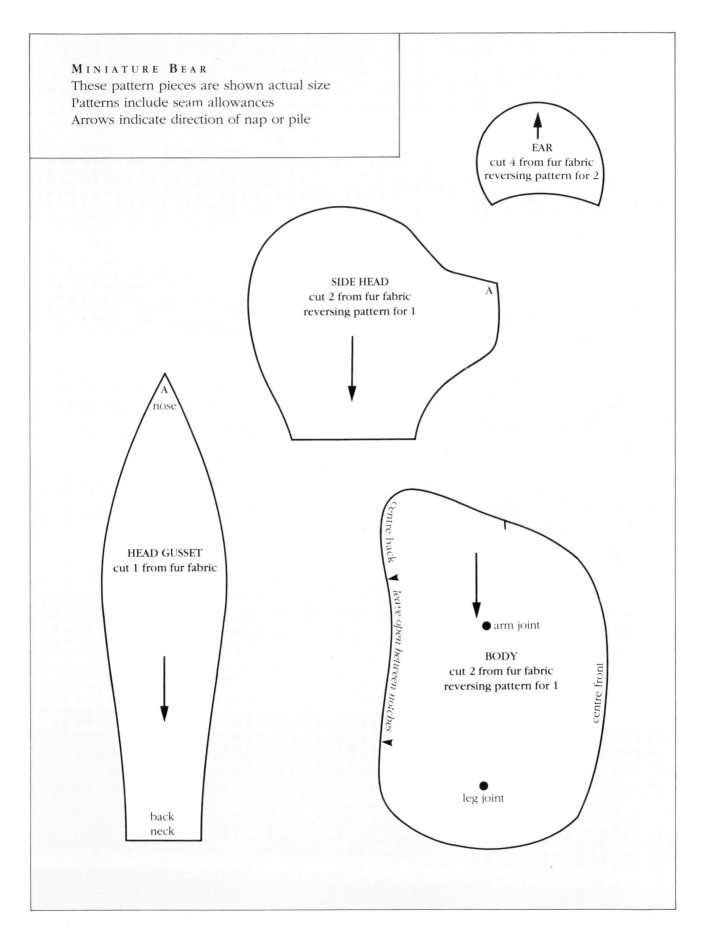

MINIATURE BEAR
These pattern pieces are shown actual size
Patterns include seam allowances
Arrows indicate direction of nap or pile

EAR
cut 4 from fur fabric
reversing pattern for 2

SIDE HEAD
cut 2 from fur fabric
reversing pattern for 1

A

A
nose

HEAD GUSSET
cut 1 from fur fabric

back
neck

centre back

leave open between notches

arm joint

BODY
cut 2 from fur fabric
reversing pattern for 1

centre front

leg joint

CLASSIC WHITE BEAR

The bear pictured here was inspired by a 1920s white bear. Made from ivory mohair pile fabric, it is 16in (40cm) tall and has ivory suedette pads.

The 1920s saw a great diversity in bear types; not least the colours and various kinds of fabrics used to make them. Shortages during the war years forced the manufacturers to experiment with a range of different materials and dyes, even though the most desirable and classic bears were still chosen from the range of mohair available.

White mohair bears are not perhaps as popular as their more usual honey-gold and brown cousins, but they do have a charm and appeal all their own.

One early white bear was produced by Steiff in 1921. This delightful bear was made from white plush and stood 15in (38cm) tall. It was of the classic shape although its legs were rather shorter than those of its predecessors. This white bear did not prove to be a huge success at the time and manufactured numbers were somewhat limited. This, of course, now makes white bears of this type extremely collectable and valuable.

Some years later, in the year 1927, Steiff manufactured a small white teddy bear called Petz. This bear is being produced again by Steiff as one in their successful replica range.

Apart from teddy bears, there have also been a large number of lookalike polar bears. In Britain, toy polar bears dating from the early 1950s were based on real life animals in the zoo. Two well known examples include Ivy and her son Brumas, polar bears then living at the London Zoo.

Early Australian bears were made in a variety of colours, including white. These white bears often had blue glass eyes, giving them an almost human expression.

Over the years, many firms across the world have produced white teddy bears. In more recent years, white teddies seem to have grown in popularity with many bear ranges including more than one white-fur variety.

Keeping needlework clean is important whatever the task. However, when working with white mohair, it is absolutely essential. Following these simple guidelines will enable you to keep your fabric in the best possible condition throughout the sewing process.

This 15in (38in) bear is probably a 1930s Chiltern.

Materials

½yd (45cm) of 54in (137cm) wide ivory mohair with ⅜in (9mm) pile

Small square of ivory-coloured suedette

Tacking (basting) thread

Matching sewing thread

Matching heavy-duty thread

One 2in (50mm) hardboard crown joint

Four 1⅜in (35mm) hardboard crown joints

Small amount of 'firm-fill' polyester filling (stuffing)

1lb (450g) wood wool

Two ⁷⁄₁₆in (11mm) black glass boot button eyes

One skein light terracotta 'stranded cotton' embroidery thread

Before beginning to cut out the fabric, lay it face downwards on a clean pillow case. Cut it out using sharp-pointed scissors, picking up the fabric away from the pillow case as you work. When all the pieces have been cut, these can then be stored away in the pillow case, which can also be used as a table or lap cover when work is actually in progress.

No matter how carefully you work, fur fabric will shed some pile during handling. This is particularly noticeable with white and other pastel colours, so a lap cover serves the dual purpose of keeping the fabric clean and preventing loose pile from covering your clothes.

The ivory bear featured here is similar in style to the bear produced in the Steiff factory during the 1920s. However, it has small black boot button eyes, giving it a somewhat quizzical expression. In the traditional manner its nose has been embroidered in a rectangle of vertical satin stitches using a terracotta embroidery thread. The same thread has been used to embroider claws which are stitched across the fur fabric onto the pad itself.

MAKING THE CLASSIC WHITE BEAR

Before starting to make the bear, carefully read the chapter on Classic Bear-making. Following the step-by-step instructions there, make the 10 templates, cut out the fabric pieces and assemble the bear, taking into consideration the special points below. Take care to keep your working surfaces as clean as possible at all times.

When drawing around templates, it is absolutely essential to ensure that the inked markings will not transfer from the surface of the templates to the fabric and a sharp, soft lead pencil should be used to draw around each shape as lightly as possible.

Small black glass eyes have been used for the bear featured here, but you may like to try coloured eyes, blue in particular, for a different expression. Larger eyes will give your bear a more wide-awake and innocent look.

The teddy bear's eyes here are placed just below the head gusset seam, so that their lower edges are 1¼in (3cm) from the centre of the tip of the bear's muzzle.

The ears should be set so that they start at the gusset seam with the lower edges tilting backwards a little.

The nose is worked with six strands of stranded cotton in vertical satin stitches across the seam at the end of the muzzle, forming a rectangle about ¾in (2cm) wide and ½in (12mm) deep. Each side of the mouth is worked downwards from the centre of the nose in two short stitches to form a slight curve.

Four claws have been embroidered on each pad using six strands of stranded cotton embroidery thread. Insert the needle through the paw at the seamline and take it to the position for working the first claw about ½in (12mm) away from the seam into the fur fabric. Pull the thread through until the tail lies within the paw itself and make a straight stitch across the seamline to ½in (12mm) across the pad. Take the needle back through the paw to the stitching position for the second claw and repeat the process until four claws have been made. Take the needle back through the paw to the seamline, pull firmly and cut the thread. The tail should then disappear into the paw, leaving a neat and tidy finish.

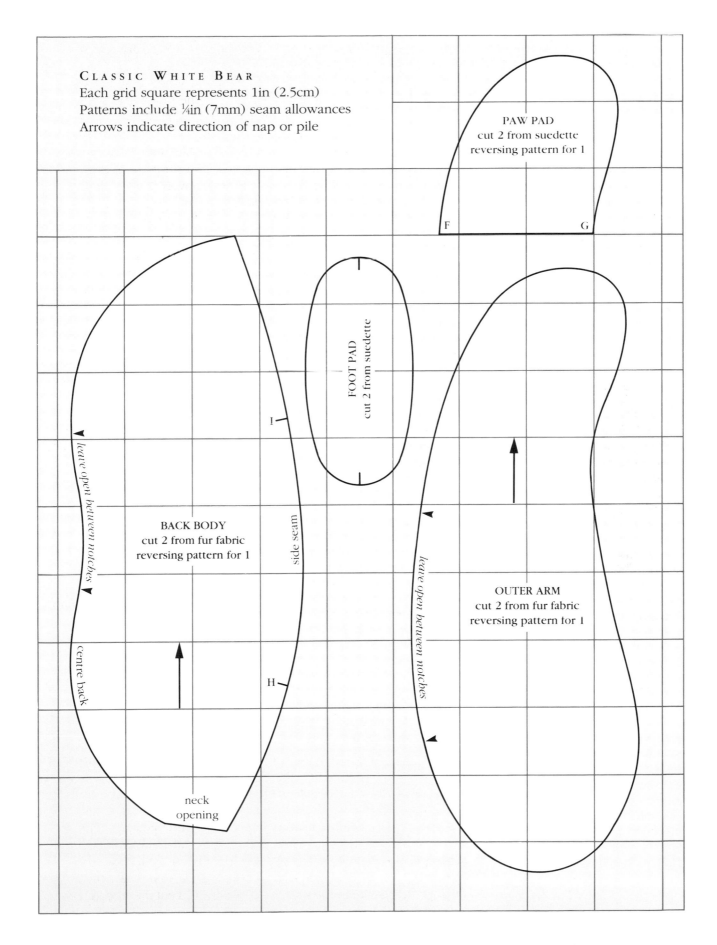

CLASSIC WHITE BEAR
Each grid square represents 1in (2.5cm)
Patterns include ¼in (7mm) seam allowances
Arrows indicate direction of nap or pile

PAW PAD
cut 2 from suedette
reversing pattern for 1

F   G

FOOT PAD
cut 2 from suedette

leave open between notches

BACK BODY
cut 2 from fur fabric
reversing pattern for 1

side seam

centre back

leave open between notches

OUTER ARM
cut 2 from fur fabric
reversing pattern for 1

H

I

neck
opening

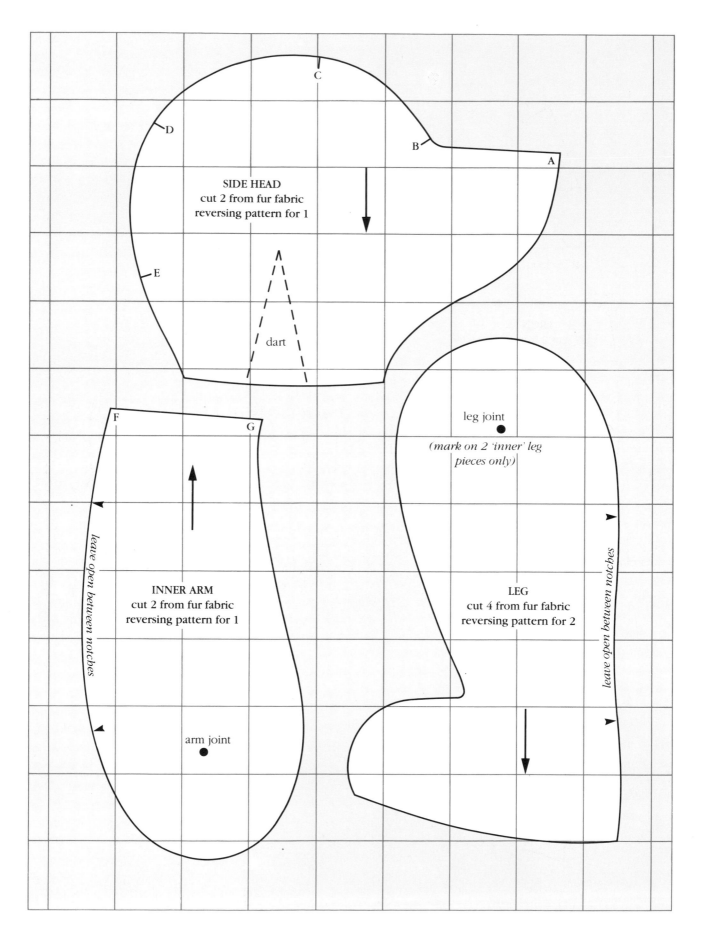

SIDE HEAD
cut 2 from fur fabric
reversing pattern for 1

dart

INNER ARM
cut 2 from fur fabric
reversing pattern for 1

arm joint

leg joint

(mark on 2 'inner' leg
pieces only)

LEG
cut 4 from fur fabric
reversing pattern for 2

leave open between notches

leave open between notches

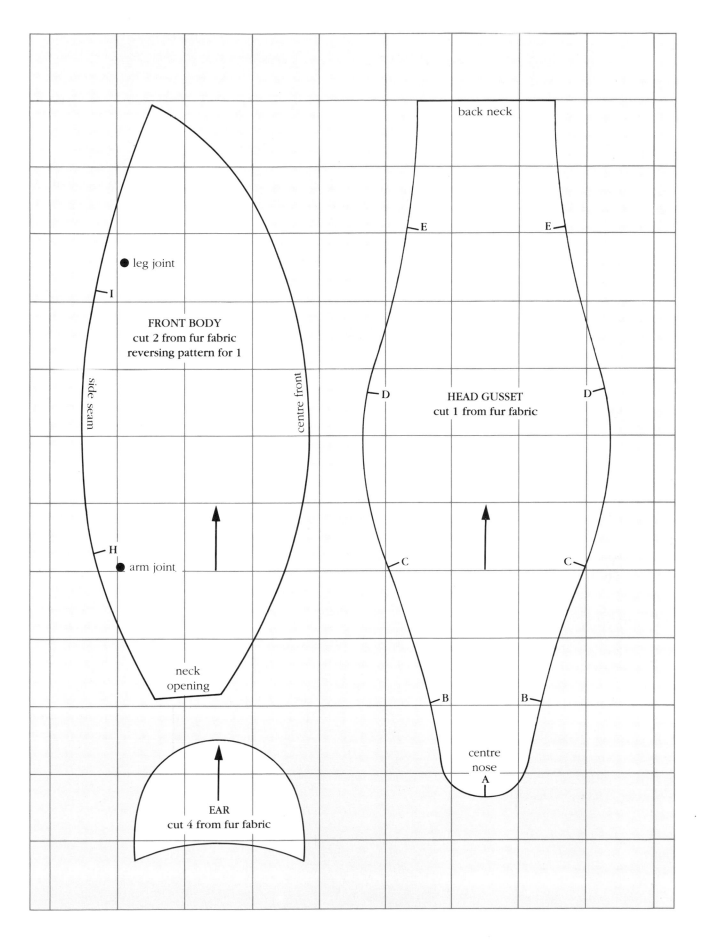

back neck

E   E

leg joint

I

FRONT BODY
cut 2 from fur fabric
reversing pattern for 1

D   HEAD GUSSET   D
cut 1 from fur fabric

side seam

centre front

H

arm joint

C   C

neck
opening

B   B

centre
nose
A

EAR
cut 4 from fur fabric

1930s BEAR

The bear pictured here was inspired by 1930s English bears. Made from fawn distressed pile mohair fabric, it is 28in (71cm) tall and has dark chocolate brown velvet paw and foot pads.

As 1930 dawned, the British teddy bear industry saw the genesis of a new company, Merrythought. Founded by C J Rendel of Chad Valley and A C Janisch of J K Farnell, Merrythought was established with the help of a mohair company – Holmes and Laxton – in Shropshire, central England. The shrewd mohair spinners were only too well aware of the growing threat from synthetic fibres to their industry; they saw teddy bear manufacture as a way to survival.

Merrythought's trademark is a wishbone (merrythought is an old English term meaning wishbone) which was imprinted on a celluloid button and sewn to the ear or the shoulder of the bear. Later the bears were labelled on the undersides of their feet.

Alongside Dean's and Chad Valley, the Merrythought Company flourished.

English bears had a generally softer outline and rounder form than their German counterparts. By the 1930s their pads were being made from Rexine, a simulated leather fabric.

Other popular teddy bears of the day were those made for the department stores and mail order catalogues. As these were produced en masse, they never had a lasting, formal identification mark label like the Merrythought or Steiff bears, so it is now difficult to trace their origins. However, the Chiltern Company, founded in the 1920s, almost certainly made a substantial number of these bears. The department store and mail order bear came in a wide array of sizes and colours.

Merrythought produced a successful range of dressed bears called Bingie bears. These 1930s novelty bears often wore extravagant costumes. Their ears were lined with a new synthetic fabric called silk plush.

Although many of the teddy bear manufacturers thrived in the 1930s, J K Farnell sadly ceased production in 1934 owing to a big fire which devastated the factory.

By the close of the decade, World War II had begun and although many manufacturers were still in production, teddies were being replaced in the factories by more essential items. Then home-made bears made from all manner of fabrics and oddments began to appear.

The bear featured on the cover of this book is an early Merrythought teddy, purchased in the 1930s. It is 28in (70cm) tall and is fitted with a growler, which, sadly, no longer works. Over the years it has given and received much love and its fur in places has worn very thin! This bear is a delightful example of the pleasure to be gained from bears of all shapes and sizes.

MAKING THE 1930S BEAR

Before starting to make the bear, carefully read the chapter on Classic Bear-making. Following the step-by-step instructions there, make the 10 templates, cut out the fabric pieces and assemble the bear, taking into consideration the special points below. Take care to keep your working surfaces as clean as possible at all times.

As this bear is quite large, it is advisable to use heavy-duty thread for all machine stitched seams.

The centre head gusset of this bear is in two sections. Cut these out as a pair, turning over the template to produce a 'pair' of pattern pieces. Join the centre seam before attaching the gusset to the side-of-head pieces in the usual manner.

Before turning the head right side out, trim the side head and centre gusset seams around the muzzle. The head should then be stuffed and closed around the hardboard joint.

The leg templates are turned over along the back seamline to produce the pattern piece, so only two leg sections are cut. The stuffing opening in this case is on the front of the leg as there is no back seam.

As the distance from the ear position to the eye socket is too far to insert a bodkin, use a doubled, knotted length of heavy-duty thread, which should be inserted close to the final placing of the eye (about 2½in (6cm) from the nose tip along the side head gusset seam). Make a few very tiny oversewing (overcasting) stitches before bringing the bodkin out a little way from these. Enlarge the hole using a bodkin, thread on the eye loop and insert the eye. Take the bodkin across the muzzle to the approximate position of the second eye, pull the thread tightly and make a few more tiny oversewing (overcasting) stitches. Make a hole and insert the eye. Then take the bodkin to the tip of the nose, finishing off with oversewing (overcasting) stitches and snipping the tail thread closely. (These stitches will be covered by the embroidery stitches of the nose.)

The nose is a rectangle of vertical satin stitches measuring 1¼in (3cm) across and 1in (2.5cm) deep and is worked using six strands of stranded cotton. The edges are neatened with several horizontal straight stitches at the top and bottom.

The smiling mouth is formed from a few straight stitches, the horizontals of which are looped upwards slightly to form a smile.

An optional growler has been inserted in this bear. If you wish to include a voice, instructions can be found on page 27.

Materials

1yd (90cm) of 54in (137cm) wide fawn distressed pile mohair with ¾in (21mm) pile

Small square of dark chocolate brown velvet

Tacking (basting) thread

Matching heavy-duty sewing thread

One 3in (76mm) hardboard crown joint

Four 3½in (88mm) hardboard crown joints

1lb (450 g) kapok

2¼lb (1kg) wood wool

Two ⅝in (15mm) amber and black glass eyes

One large deep-voiced growler (optional)

Scrap of calico or muslin for growler (optional)

One skein black 'stranded cotton' embroidery thread

A 1930s Merrythought label.

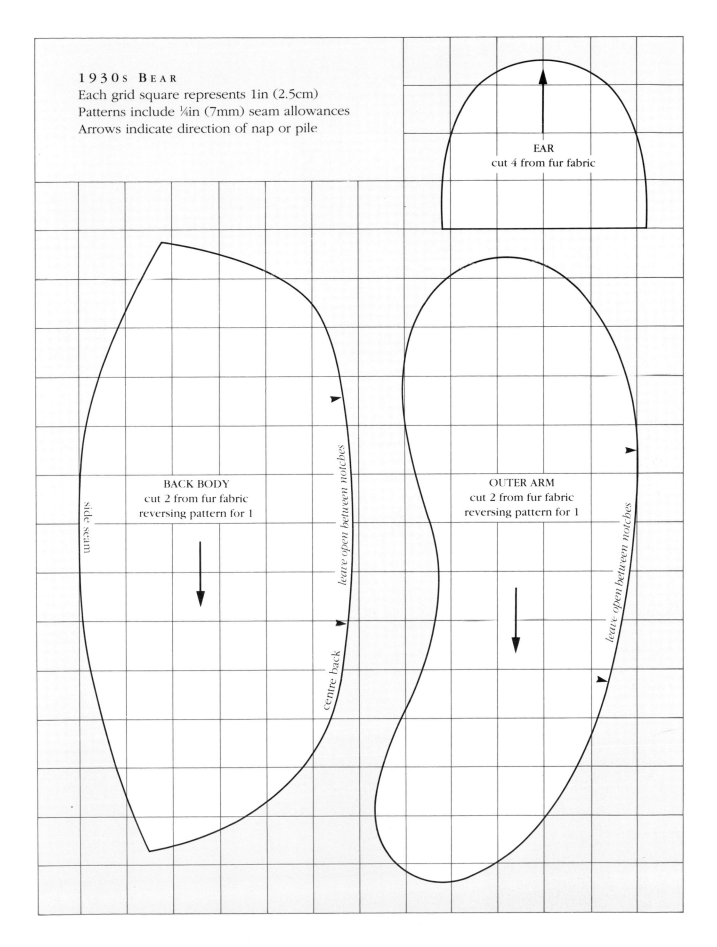

1930S BEAR
Each grid square represents 1in (2.5cm)
Patterns include ¼in (7mm) seam allowances
Arrows indicate direction of nap or pile

EAR
cut 4 from fur fabric

BACK BODY
cut 2 from fur fabric
reversing pattern for 1

side seam

centre back

leave open between notches

OUTER ARM
cut 2 from fur fabric
reversing pattern for 1

leave open between notches

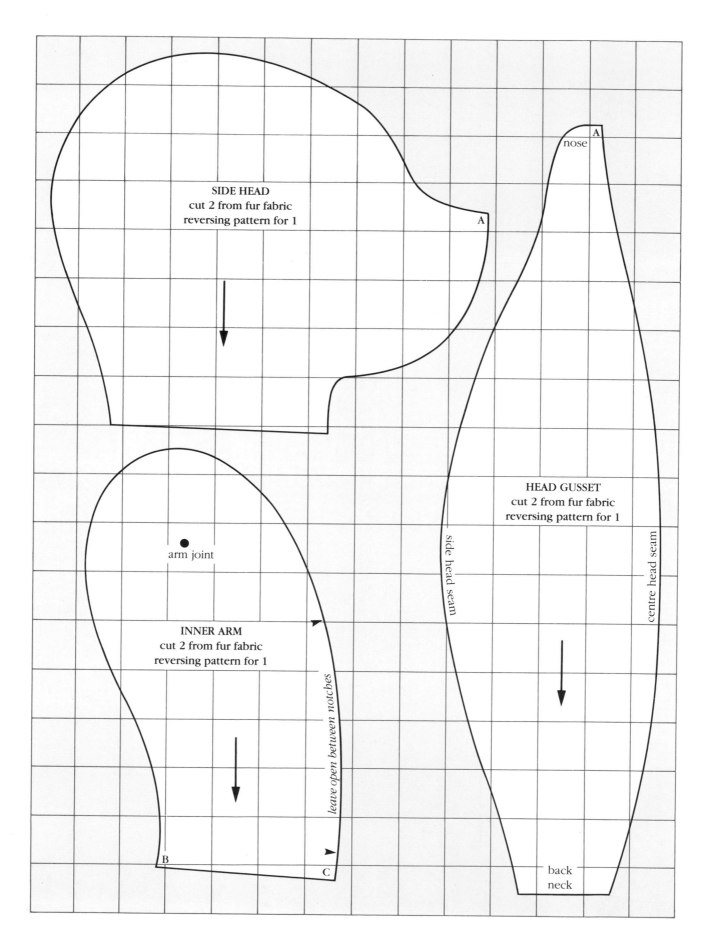

SIDE HEAD
cut 2 from fur fabric
reversing pattern for 1

A

nose A

HEAD GUSSET
cut 2 from fur fabric
reversing pattern for 1

side head seam

centre head seam

arm joint

INNER ARM
cut 2 from fur fabric
reversing pattern for 1

leave open between notches

B C

back
neck

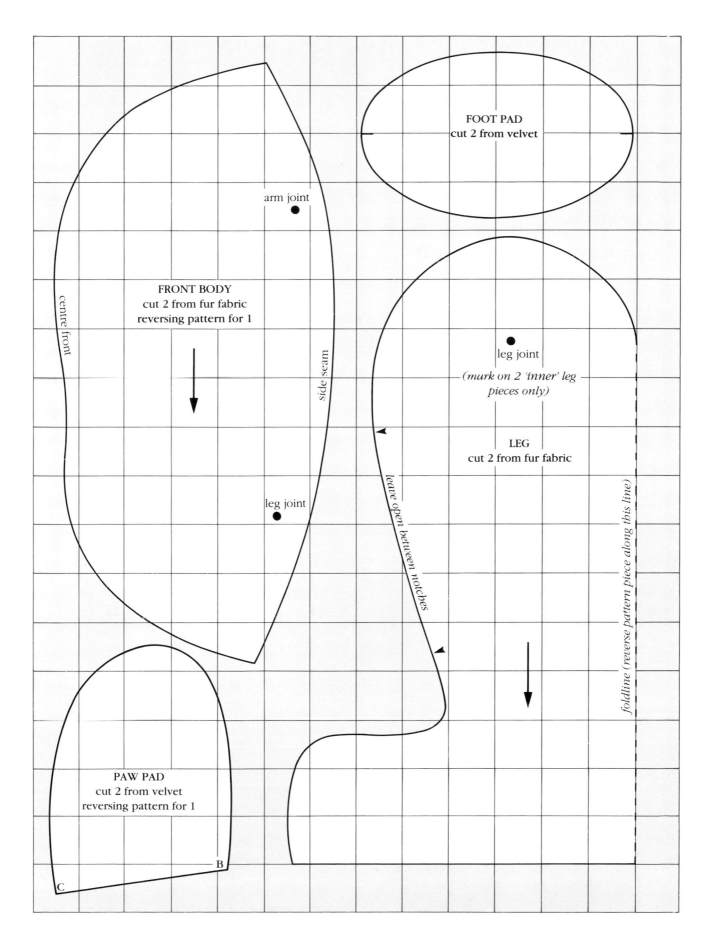

FOOT PAD
cut 2 from velvet

arm joint

FRONT BODY
cut 2 from fur fabric
reversing pattern for 1

centre front

side seam

leg joint

(mark on 'inner' leg pieces only)

leg joint

leave open between notches

LEG
cut 2 from fur fabric

foldline (reverse pattern piece along this line)

PAW PAD
cut 2 from velvet
reversing pattern for 1

B

C

FRENCH BEAR

Until World War I most bears sold in France, as in Britain, were imported from Germany. However, as the conflict continued, a small, but nevertheless significant domestic industry set about manufacturing teddy bears.

Generally, French bears were not of such high quality as German models; fur was usually a lower standard – being harsher and more bristly. It was also often a brasher, brighter gold. Later on, in the 1930s, many bears were made from an inferior artificial plush.

The most notable thing about the French teddy was its appearance. Being less substantial than its German counterpart, it tended to have much thinner arms and legs, as well as a shorter muzzle. Bodies were also often slimmer and straighter than other bears, especially if compared with quality Steiff or Hermann teddies.

Jointing on French teddies was also very different as a cruder exterior wire system was used which, when the fabric disintegrated, meant the bear really did fall to pieces. Eyes were usually clear glass, hand-painted on the back in black or brown. These were often held in place with glue or fastened singly by means of a wire loop.

As the French tended to favour dolls, teddy bear manufacture never took off like it did in Britain, the United States, Germany or even Eastern Europe.

As French bears were generally constructed in an inferior way, few good bear examples from the early part of the century exist.

One noted French producer was M Pintel Fils & Cie. Bears from this and similar factories can be identified by a trade button, rather like the famous Steiff mark, on the chest or ear.

The French are probably better known for their mechanical bears, some excellent examples of which still exist from around the 1920s.

Because of the French bears' rather slimmer shape, they make an interesting alternative to sew. This bear is made from a honey-gold mohair, although one of the bright new colours could be used as a substitute. The pads are dark beige suedette and the eyes are cheeky little boot buttons.

A little experience of making teddy bears will show that no two bears look exactly the same. The slightest variation in the positioning of the ears or eyes will produce a very different character from the

ones shown in the photographs in this book. One of the pleasures of making classic bears is that, as they are assembled, they take on their own particular personality. You will soon decide just how you like your bear to look.

Traditionally, bears have been given an inverted Y shaped mouth, but even within this guideline, there are endless variations of expression. Should the fur pile cause long stitches to shift position, hold them down with a few tiny straight anchoring stitches.

Most early bears have small eyes which are rather close-set. Placing eyes further apart will give a wide-eyed and innocent look. In general, teddy bears' eyes look best set low down on the head, not too far from the muzzle, but this again is a matter of preference. A rather vacant expression can be achieved by moving the eyes further towards the ears, spacing them widely apart.

Materials

¼yd (25cm) of 54in (137cm)
* wide honey-gold mohair*
* with ⅜in (9mm) pile*
Small square of dark beige
* suedette*
Tacking (basting) thread
Matching sewing thread
Matching heavy-duty thread
One 2in (50mm) hardboard
* crown joint*
Four 1⅜in (36mm)
* hardboard crown joints*
Small amount of 'firm-fill'
* polyester filling (stuffing)*
1lb (450g) wood wool
Two ½in (12mm) black glass
* boot button eyes*
One skein black 'soft cotton'
* embroidery thread*

MAKING THE FRENCH BEAR

Before starting to make the bear, carefully read the chapter on Classic Bear-making. Following the step-by-step instructions there, make the 10 templates, cut out the fabric pieces and assemble the bear, taking into consideration the special points below. Take care to keep your working surfaces as clean as possible at all times.

Stuff the muzzle firmly, using polyester filling (stuffing), to form a short, angular shape.

The eyes should be placed on the head seam, so that their lower edges are about 1¾ (4.5cm) from the tip of the muzzle.

The ears should be set vertically downwards from the head gusset seams on the sides of the head 1¾in (4.5cm) from the eye position. The top tip of each ear should just be touching the head gusset seam.

The nose is worked in horizontal satin stitches, following the tip of the head gusset seamlines and forming a blunt-ended triangle which finishes just below the point of the head gusset seam.

From the centre of the lower edge of the nose, make a ½in (12mm) straight stitch downwards, following the lower seamline and using two strands of soft cotton thread. The mouth is then formed by making a ¾in (18mm) straight stitch from the centre to the right, back to the centre and a ¾in (18mm) straight stitch from the centre to the left. The expression of your bear can be altered by varying the angle of these straight stitches. Upturned stitches will express a contented bear, while downturned stitches will portray a need to be cuddled!

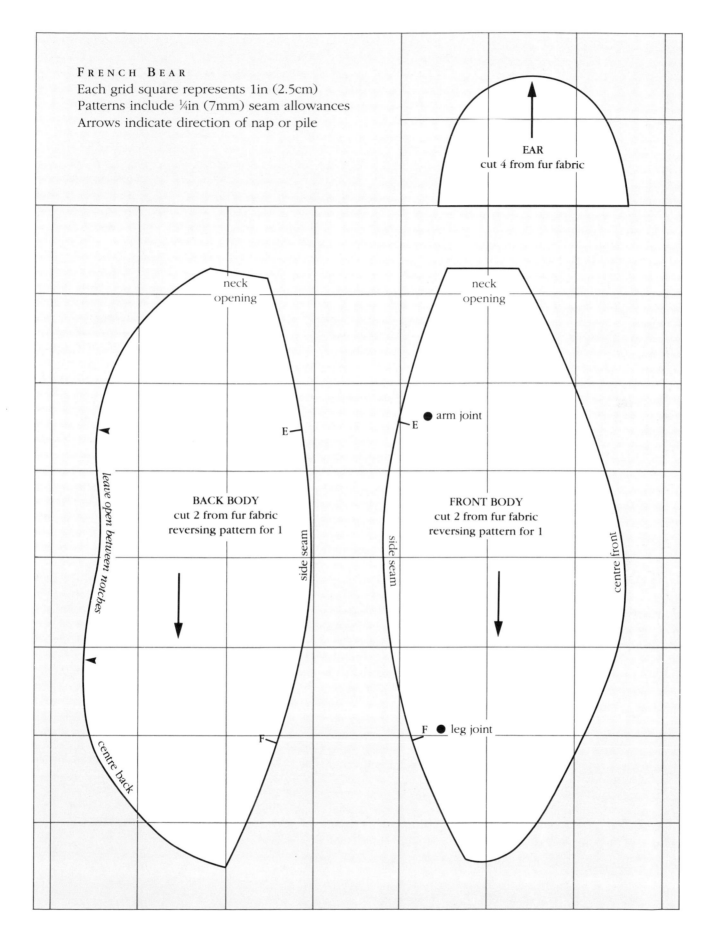

FRENCH BEAR
Each grid square represents 1in (2.5cm)
Patterns include ¼in (7mm) seam allowances
Arrows indicate direction of nap or pile

EAR
cut 4 from fur fabric

neck
opening

neck
opening

● arm joint

E

E

BACK BODY
cut 2 from fur fabric
reversing pattern for 1

FRONT BODY
cut 2 from fur fabric
reversing pattern for 1

leave open between notches

side seam

side seam

centre front

centre back

F

F ● leg joint

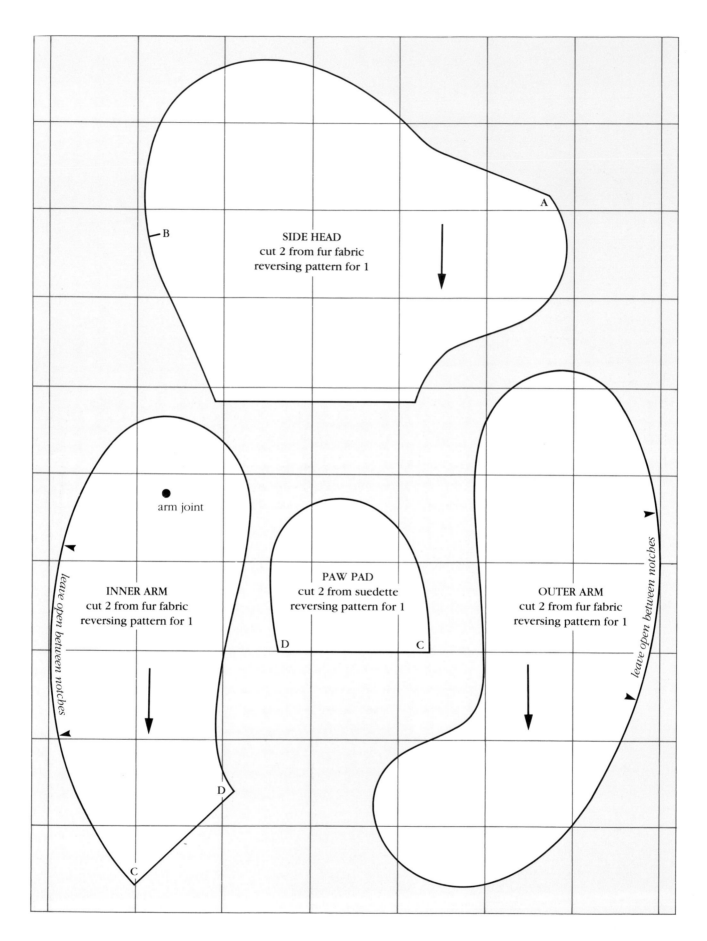

SIDE HEAD
cut 2 from fur fabric
reversing pattern for 1

A

B

arm joint

INNER ARM
cut 2 from fur fabric
reversing pattern for 1

leave open between notches

PAW PAD
cut 2 from suedette
reversing pattern for 1

D   C

OUTER ARM
cut 2 from fur fabric
reversing pattern for 1

leave open between notches

D

C

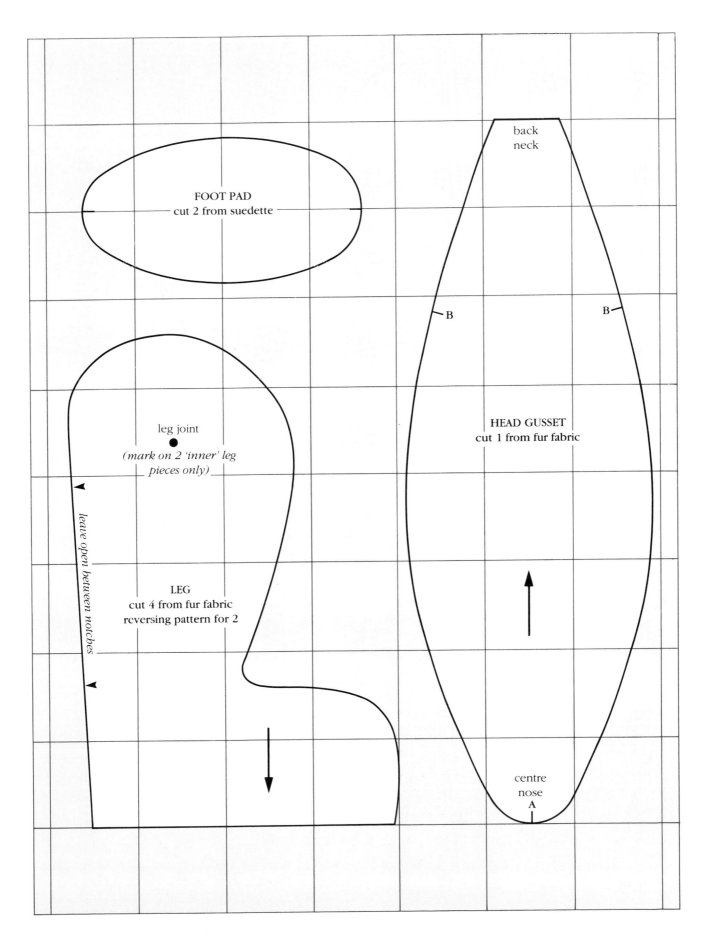

FOOT PAD
cut 2 from suedette

back
neck

B

B

leg joint

(mark on 2 'inner' leg
pieces only)

HEAD GUSSET
cut 1 from fur fabric

leave open between notches

LEG
cut 4 from fur fabric
reversing pattern for 2

centre
nose
A

WARTIME BEAR

During World War II, imports were once again restricted. In the early part of the war, the domestic markets boomed. In Britain, firms such as Chad Valley, Chiltern and Merrythought took advantage of the lack of competition from the mainly German factories. But as the conflict dragged on, supplies for toy manufacture diminished, even though the best mohair fabrics were produced in Yorkshire. Many smaller manufacturers which had been formed to meet the demand for teddy bears over the previous fifteen or so years, were forced to close down.

However, teddy bears continued to be made. As stocks on the shelves dwindled, publishers were quick to respond to the demands of needlewomen and produced instruction books for making a variety of soft toys. Patterns also appeared in women's magazines and newspapers. One publication stressed the therapeutic value of creative handiwork, recommending the satisfaction to be derived from producing a cuddly toy from the contents of a rag bag!

Some of the more unlikely materials suggested for recycling were moth-eaten swimming costumes, old vests and discarded hats. Old stockings and cotton fabrics were shredded to form the filling, while buttons and old leather gloves were recommended for creating the features.

Many much-loved bears exist from this time. Some were made from old blankets or coats. Others wore hand-knitted clothes. Because of the shortage of fur fabric, the bodies of some bears were made from clothing fabric while what little fur was available was saved for the head, paws and feet.

In other parts of the world, bears were being put together from equally unusual bits and pieces. Australia's small manufacturing industry turned out teddies made from sheepskin, a readily available material.

This bear is based on a style popular during World War II, but it has been made in a traditional short-pile mohair fabric. Its nose, however, has been cut from leather salvaged from a pair of soft leather gloves. The pattern could also be used to make a bear from an old cashmere or wool coat in line with the wartime 'make do and mend' spirit.

As with all the patterns in this book, the materials used have been listed for your convenience and guidance, but with a little experience, a variety of different fabrics can be used with any of the patterns to produce bears with very different characteristics and expressions. Try taking the ear shape from one bear and the eye

Materials

*¼yd (25cm) of 54in (137cm)
wide honey-gold mohair
with ⅜in (9mm) pile*

*Small square of dark beige
suedette*

Tacking (basting) thread

Matching sewing thread

Matching heavy-duty thread

*One 1⅜in (36mm)
hardboard crown joint*

*Four 1in (25mm) hardboard
crown joints*

*Small amount of 'firm-fill'
polyester filling (stuffing)*

1lb (450 g) wood wool

*Two ½in (12mm) amber
glass eyes*

*Small scrap of fine dark
brown leather or felt*

*One skein dark brown
'stranded cotton'
embroidery thread*

A 12in (30cm) 1940s bear.

position from another to achieve a variety of permutations. Or change an arm or body shape to produce your own individual friend. Before cutting the precious fabric, however, fit together the templates to build the basic bear shape. You will soon be able to judge quite accurately the finished effect of your bear by assessing the cardboard cut-outs.

MAKING THE WARTIME BEAR

Before starting to make the bear, carefully read the chapter on Classic Bear-making. Following the step-by-step instructions there, make the 10 templates, cut out the fabric pieces and assemble the bear, taking into consideration the special points below. Take care to keep your working surfaces as clean as possible at all times.

The front and back leg sections on this particular bear are cut in one piece which is then folded over to form a single back seam. When cutting the legs out, cut two pieces, remembering to turn the pattern piece over and to reverse all the markings to form a 'pair' of legs.

The feet are formed from separate crescent-shaped sections which are attached before the back seam is stitched. Do take care to match the notches correctly. The half moon should sit centrally along the lower straight edge of the leg, and should be eased slightly to fit. There will be a small space on either side of the leg section. This is to accommodate the seam allowance. Tack (baste) and machine stitch the foot in place, before closing the back seam. The foot pad can then be positioned in the usual way.

The four arm pieces are cut from a single pattern piece. Again do remember to draw two sections, before turning over the template to draw the second pair. The suedette pads are slip stitched into position (turning a tiny hem) when the arms are completed, but before they are attached to the body.

Position the eyes just wide of the head gusset seam about 1¼in (3cm) from the nose tip. The inner edge of the eyes should sit just on the seamline on each side of the head.

Stitch the inner third of each ear along the head gusset seam, starting about 1¾in (4.5cm) from the top of the eye and working towards the back of the head. When the back seam of the ear has been secured, twist the remaining two-thirds downwards vertically and stitch in place. Complete the front seam of the ear in the normal way.

The nose on this bear has been cut from a small scrap of glove leather. If this is not available, felt can be used. Trim away a little of the fur pile at the tip of the muzzle before attaching the nose using a matching thread and small straight stitches. The mouth has been embroidered with straight stitches, using six strands of brown stranded cotton. The centre stitch following the muzzle seam and each of the two branches forming the mouth are all ¼in (7mm) long.

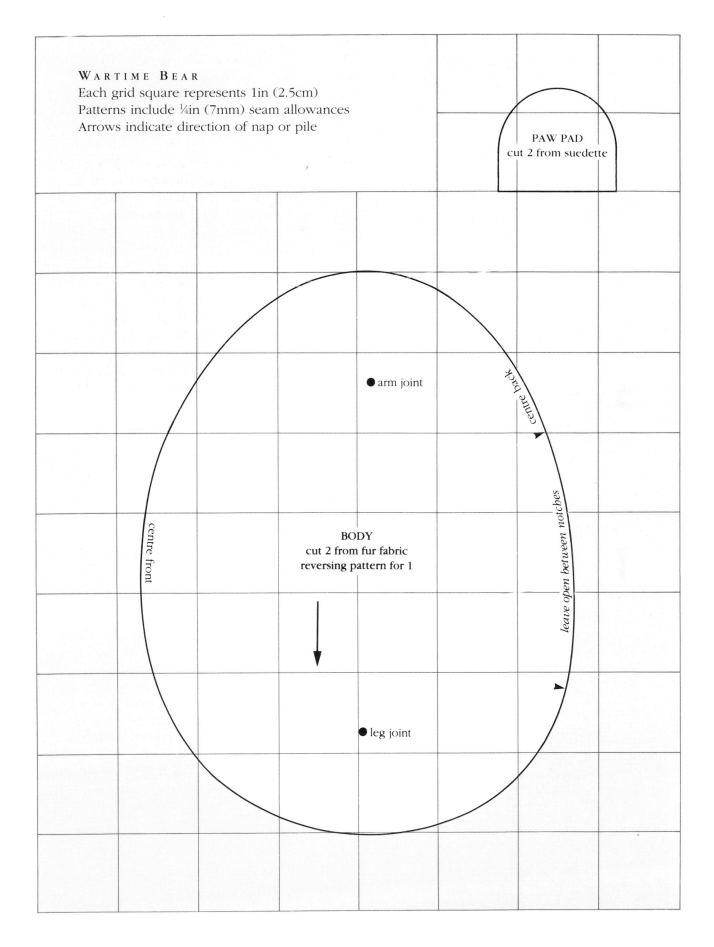

WARTIME BEAR
Each grid square represents 1in (2.5cm)
Patterns include ¼in (7mm) seam allowances
Arrows indicate direction of nap or pile

PAW PAD
cut 2 from suedette

● arm joint

centre back

centre front

leave open between notches

BODY
cut 2 from fur fabric
reversing pattern for 1

● leg joint

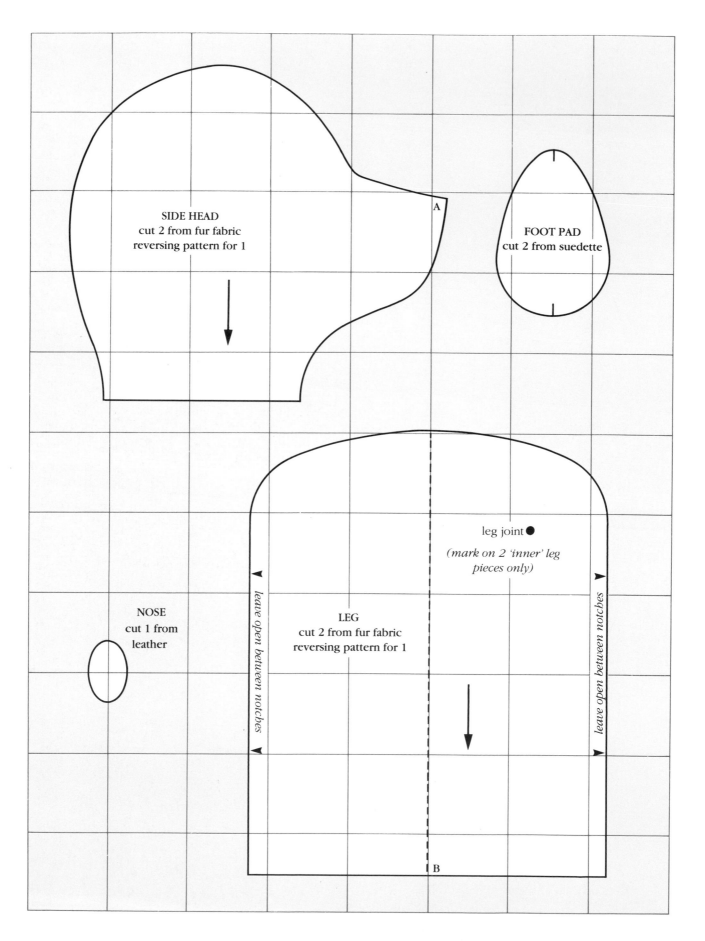

SIDE HEAD
cut 2 from fur fabric
reversing pattern for 1

A

FOOT PAD
cut 2 from suedette

NOSE
cut 1 from
leather

LEG
cut 2 from fur fabric
reversing pattern for 1

leave open between notches

leave open between notches

leg joint ●

(mark on 2 'inner' leg pieces only)

B

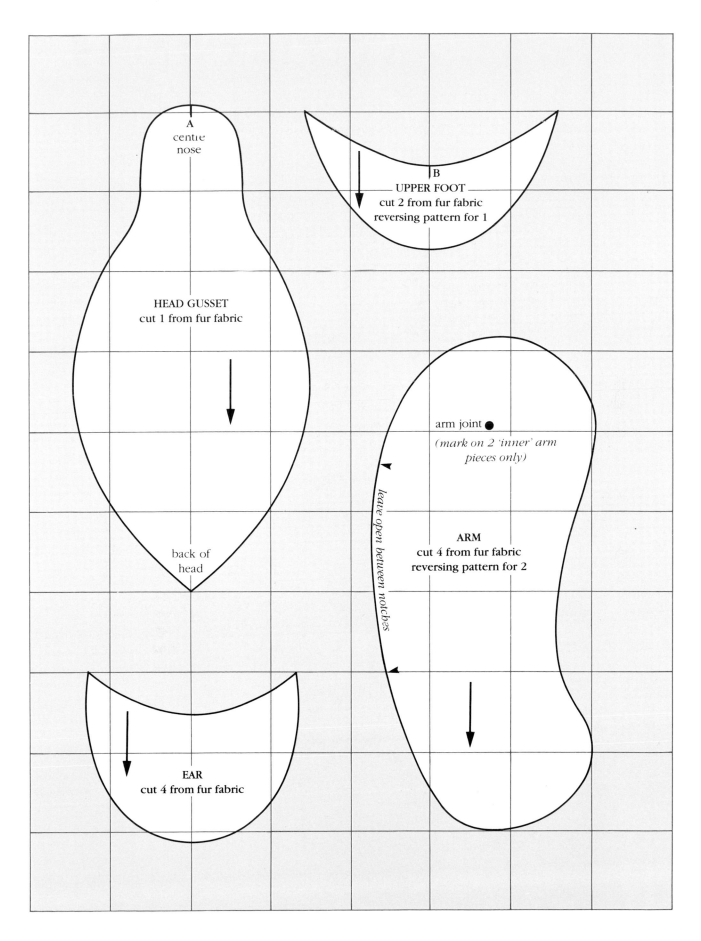

A
centre
nose

B
UPPER FOOT
cut 2 from fur fabric
reversing pattern for 1

HEAD GUSSET
cut 1 from fur fabric

arm joint ●
(mark on 2 'inner' arm
pieces only)

back of
head

leave open between notches

ARM
cut 4 from fur fabric
reversing pattern for 2

EAR
cut 4 from fur fabric

AMERICAN BEAR

The bear pictured here was inspired by 1940s American bears. Made from gold fur fabric, it is 14in (36cm) tall and has dark beige suedette paw and foot pads.

The years between the two world wars saw an unprecedented boom in the manufacture of teddy bears.

In America, production during this time thrived. One of the more successful companies was the Knickerbocker Toy Co Inc. Originally founded in the early 1900s in New York, some of the bears from this manufacturer still survive in excellent condition.

The bear featured here is similar to the Knickerbocker bear in production around 1940. It has a typically large round head with a relatively flat, snubbed muzzle.

Bear shapes and features were continually evolving. Around this time, the body shape was changing quite dramatically. Gone was the hump; legs and arms became shorter and thicker and claws were often omitted. Stuffing was almost entirely kapok, giving a softer shape to the bear's physique. Although most bears' arms still displayed the distinctive curve of the earlier models, these new varieties were much more familiar to the teddy bears we know today.

The trademark of the Knickerbocker Toy Company at this time showed an inverted horseshoe containing the figure of a child. This could be seen on sew-in labels, usually placed in the front body seam or in the ear. Later labels were to proclaim the slogan 'Animals of Distinction'.

The Knickerbocker toy factory is still famous for its Smokey bear characters, manufactured during the 1960s and 1970s Smokey was used to promote the work of the Junior Forest rangers and the young owners were encouraged to enrol in this organization which aimed to prevent the outbreak of forest fires. Several toy companies, including The Ideal Toy Co, were also licensed to produce this popular bear, which was named after Smokey Joe Martin, an employee of the New York Fire Department in the 1920s.

Although the Knickerbocker bears, in common with most others of that time, were made from mohair fabric, this bear is made from synthetic knitted fabric and is, therefore, an ideal bear for a beginner to attempt. Synthetic fabric is relatively cheap, and so mistakes in cutting out are not so crucial, as with expensive mohair. Fabric with a knitted

backing does, however, need careful handling during the stuffing process as it may pull out of shape or distort. For this reason a light polyester filling has been used, and, as in the original bear, the arms and legs have been less firmly stuffed than is usual. Polyester filling is non-allergenic and conforms to toy safety standards. If this bear is to be made as a child's toy, plastic lock-in safety eyes must be used.

Materials
½yd (45cm) of 54in (137cm) wide gold acrylic fur fabric
Small square of dark beige suedette
Tacking (basting) thread
Matching sewing thread
Matching heavy-duty thread
One 1⅜in (36mm) hardboard crown joint
Four 1in (25mm) hardboard crown joints
1lb (450g) washable 'firm-fill' polyester filling (stuffing)
Two ½in (12mm) amber and black glass eyes
One skein black 'soft cotton' embroidery thread

MAKING THE AMERICAN BEAR
Before starting to make the bear, carefully read the chapter on Classic Bear-making. Following the step-by-step instructions there, make the 8 templates, cut out the fabric pieces and assemble the bear, taking into consideration the special points below. Take care to keep your working surfaces as clean as possible at all times.

On this bear four complete arm sections are cut out, making two pairs. These are then machine sewn together, leaving an opening between the notches for stuffing in the usual way.

The paw pads are formed from narrow ovals of dark beige suedette which are sewn in place after the side seams have been sewn, but before the arms are stuffed. The pads on the feet are large ovals, which are inserted in the usual manner.

The ears should be set at the centre of the top of the head across the gusset seams and at a slight angle with the lower edges tilting backwards a little. They are slightly padded out with a small amount of polyester filling (stuffing).

The bear's muzzle should be clipped to a neat oval, finishing just below the eyes.

Amber glass eyes with black pupils have been used and the securing thread has been pulled firmly to cause a depression for each eye socket. The eyes are placed on the head gusset seam, so that their lower edges are 1⅜in (3.5cm) from the centre of the tip of the nose.

The nose is worked in vertical satin stitches across the seam at the end of the muzzle, forming a horizontal oval about ⅞in (22mm) wide and ⅝in (16mm) deep.

The mouth is formed from three straight stitches in an inverted 'Y' shape, using soft cotton embroidery thread.

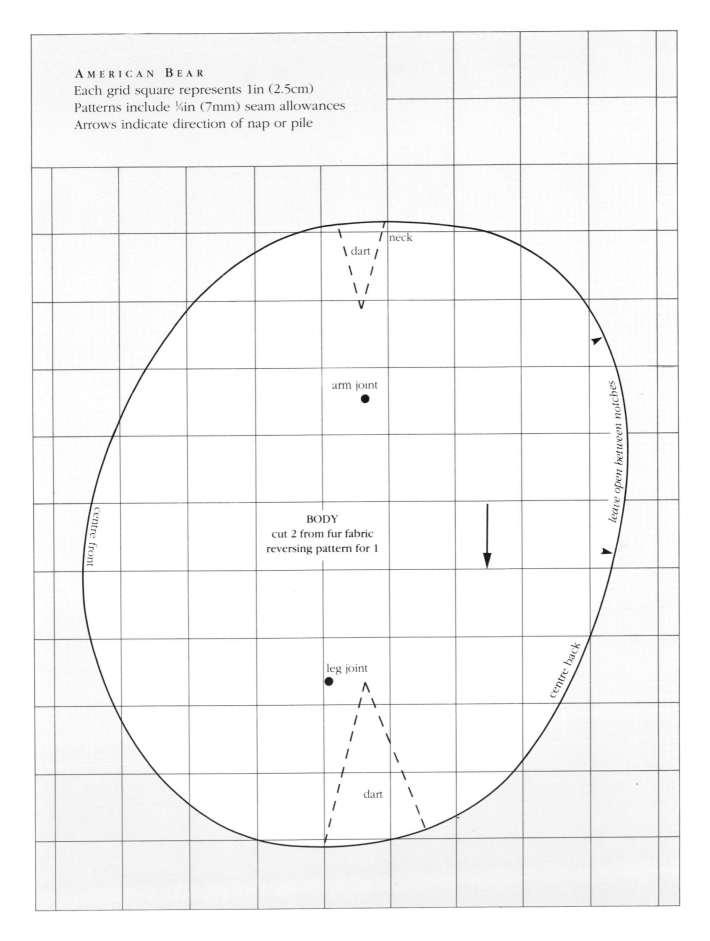

American Bear

Each grid square represents 1in (2.5cm)
Patterns include ¼in (7mm) seam allowances
Arrows indicate direction of nap or pile

dart

neck

arm joint

leave open between notches

centre front

BODY
cut 2 from fur fabric
reversing pattern for 1

centre back

leg joint

dart

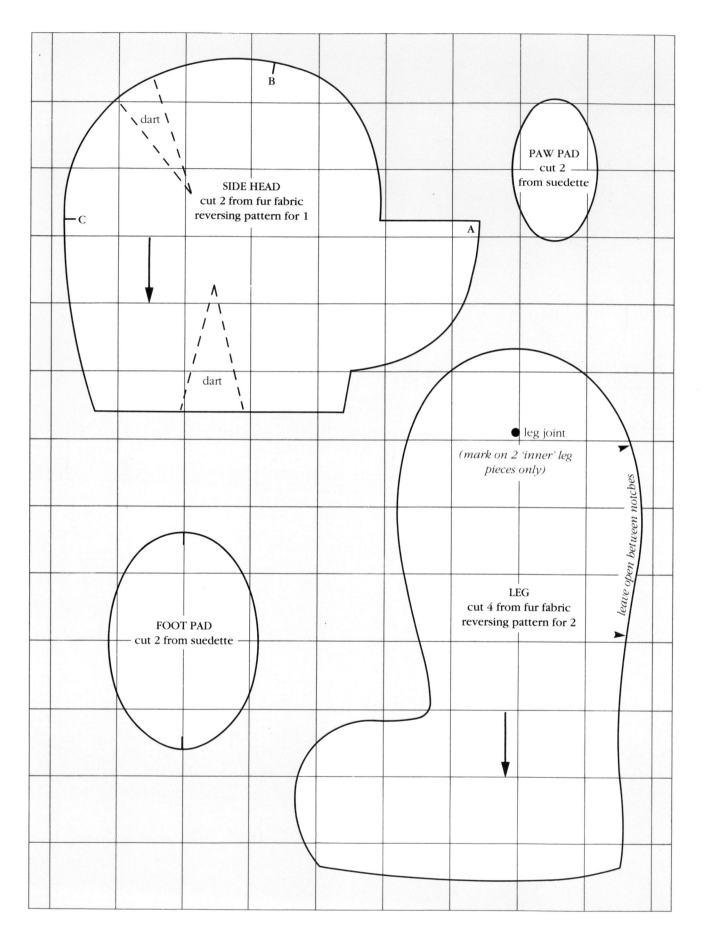

SIDE HEAD
cut 2 from fur fabric
reversing pattern for 1

dart

dart

B

C

A

PAW PAD
cut 2
from suedette

● leg joint

(mark on 2 'inner' leg
pieces only)

leave open between notches

LEG
cut 4 from fur fabric
reversing pattern for 2

FOOT PAD
cut 2 from suedette

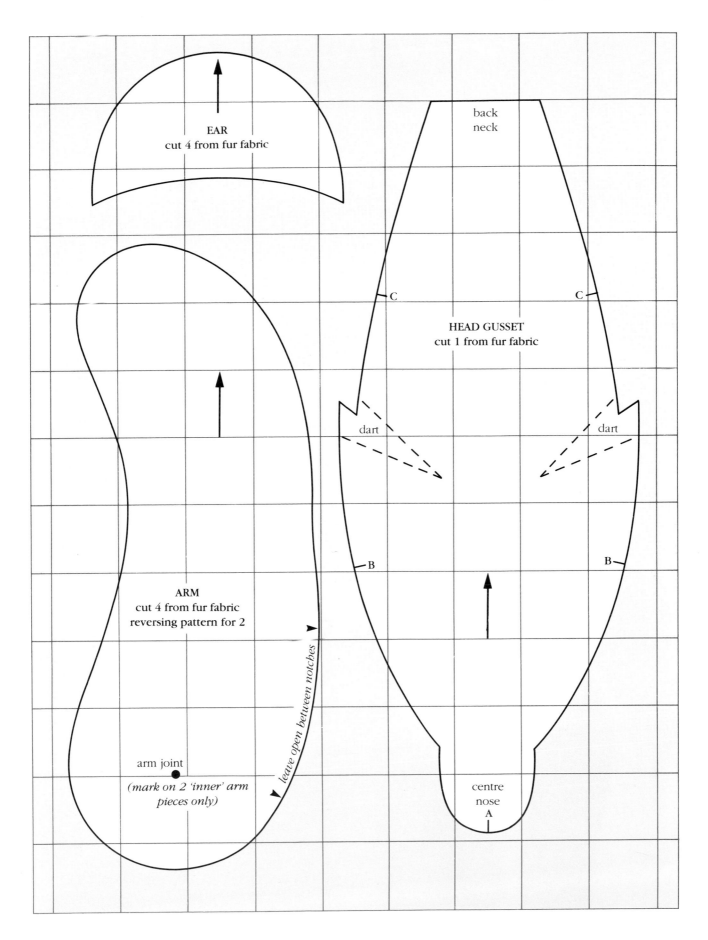

EAR
cut 4 from fur fabric

back
neck

C   C

HEAD GUSSET
cut 1 from fur fabric

dart   dart

ARM
cut 4 from fur fabric
reversing pattern for 2

B   B

leave open between notches

arm joint
●
*(mark on 2 'inner' arm
pieces only)*

centre
nose
A

CHARACTER BEAR

The bear pictured here was inspired by character bears. Made from honeysuckle mohair pile fabric, it is 14in (36cm) tall and has light beige pads.

Over the years, since the first teddy bears were developed, some of them have been characterized and thus immortalized in literature for everyone to enjoy.

As the teddy bear craze gained momentum at the beginning of the century, so teddy bears began to appear in print. The Tale of Teddy Bright-Eyes was published in Britain in 1909, teddies also appear in stories by Mrs Craddock in 1917. But it was not until the 1920s that two of the most famous bears of literature were born: Rupert and Winnie-the-Pooh.

Rupert Bear made his first appearance in Britain's *Daily Express* newspaper as a comic strip character. He was created by Mary Tourtel, a talented illustrator who was married to the paper's night editor. Rupert became an instant success and Mary Tourtel's stories set in the fictional world of Nutwood with a host of animal friends still delight children today, the world over.

When Mary retired in 1935, Rupert's adventures were taken over by Alfred Bestall who continued to submit a daily comic strip for another 30 years. As Rupert's fame continued, his adventures could be followed in annuals, cartoons, jigsaw puzzles and even in a television series.

Four years after the arrival of Rupert, Winnie-the-Pooh was to enter the arena with the publication of *When We Were Very Young*. A A Milne based his Pooh stories on his son Christopher's teddy, bought at Harrods in London one birthday. The bear – probably of Farnell manufacture – was named Edward.

It is the E H Shepard illustrations of Pooh (inspired incidentally by a different teddy – a Steiff called Growler) that will be familiar to Pooh devotees all over the world.

The original Winnie-the-Pooh now lives in the New York Public Library on Fifth Avenue.

More recently, other teddy bears have found fame in newspapers, books and television. In France, Gros Nounours began his career in newspapers during the 1960s before finding real fame on the television in a series which ran for over 1,000 episodes. Nounours' career runs parallel with the British glove puppet Sooty and the American cartoon bear, Yogi. And there are so many others: Paddington Bear, SuperTed and Carebears are known across the world.

The character bear to make here could sport a scarf in the Rupert Bear tradition. He wears tiny bells in his ears. It is made from honeysuckle-coloured short-pile mohair and has paw and foot pads of light beige.

*This 11in (28cm) tall
Winnie-the-Pooh bear was
produced in a limited edition
in 1993.*

Materials
*½yd (45cm) of 54in (137cm)
wide honeysuckle mohair
with ⅜in (9mm) pile
Small square of light beige felt
Tacking (basting) thread
Matching sewing thread
Matching heavy-duty thread
One 1⅜in (36mm)
hardboard crown joint
Four 1in (25mm) hardboard
joints
Two ⁹⁄₁₆in (15mm) amber
glass eyes
Small amount of 'firm-fill'
polyester filling (stuffing)
1lb (450 g) wood wool
One skein black 'soft cotton'
embroidery thread
Two small bells (for ears)*

MAKING THE CHARACTER BEAR

Before starting to make the bear, carefully read the chapter on Classic Bear-making. Following the step-by-step instructions there, make the 10 templates, cut out the fabric pieces and assemble the bear, taking into consideration the special points below. Take care to keep your working surfaces as clean as possible at all times.

A small bell has been placed in each ear before it is sewn in position. These will make the bear 'tinkle' gently when it is shaken. The ears have been placed slightly to the back of the head, slightly overlapping the centre head gusset on each side. The distance from the nose tip to the ear is about 4in (10cm).

The eyes are positioned just across the head gusset 2in (5cm) from the nose tip. They have been pulled in slightly to create an eye 'socket' and the fur has been trimmed away to give a wide-eyed expression.

The heart-shaped nose is worked in vertical satin stitches using black soft cotton embroidery thread.

The mouth is formed as a large inverted 'Y' following the muzzle seam. The first downwards stitch should measure about ½in (12mm) and each branch of the mouth ⅜in (1cm).

By following the pattern markings for placing the leg joints, the bear will have an endearing pigeon-toed appearance.

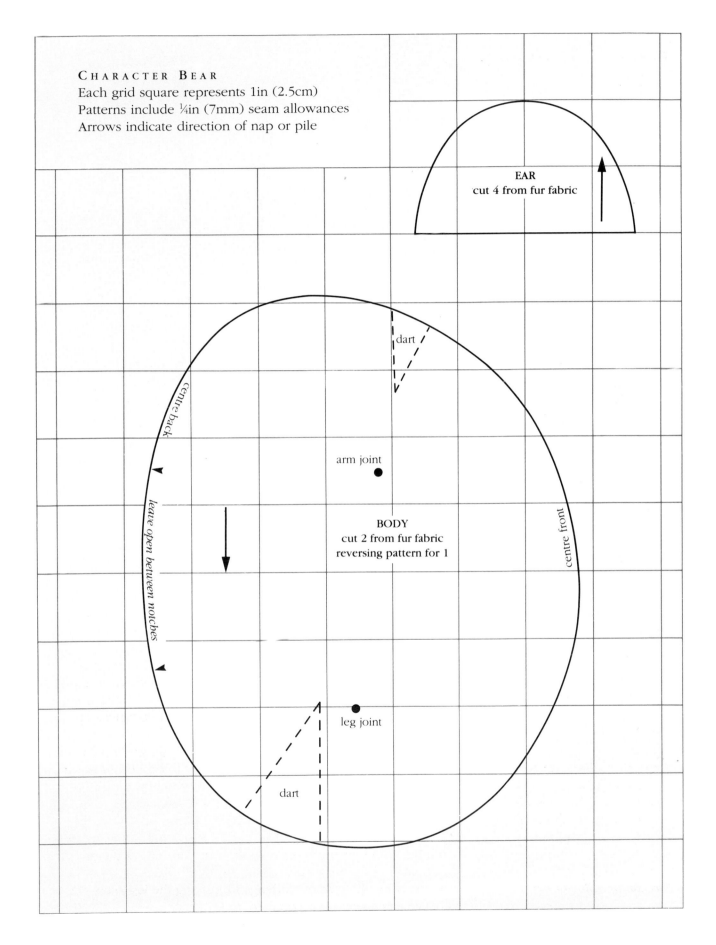

CHARACTER BEAR
Each grid square represents 1in (2.5cm)
Patterns include ¼in (7mm) seam allowances
Arrows indicate direction of nap or pile

EAR
cut 4 from fur fabric

dart

centre back

arm joint

leave open between notches

BODY
cut 2 from fur fabric
reversing pattern for 1

centre front

leg joint

dart

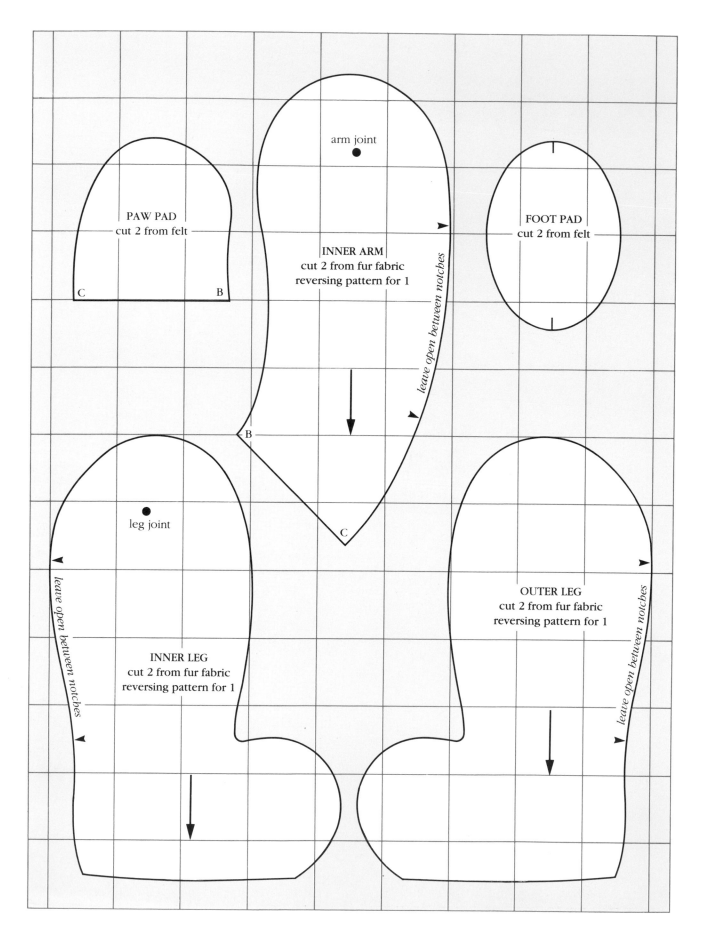

PAW PAD
cut 2 from felt

C   B

arm joint

INNER ARM
cut 2 from fur fabric
reversing pattern for 1

leave open between notches

FOOT PAD
cut 2 from felt

B

C

leg joint

leave open between notches

INNER LEG
cut 2 from fur fabric
reversing pattern for 1

OUTER LEG
cut 2 from fur fabric
reversing pattern for 1

leave open between notches

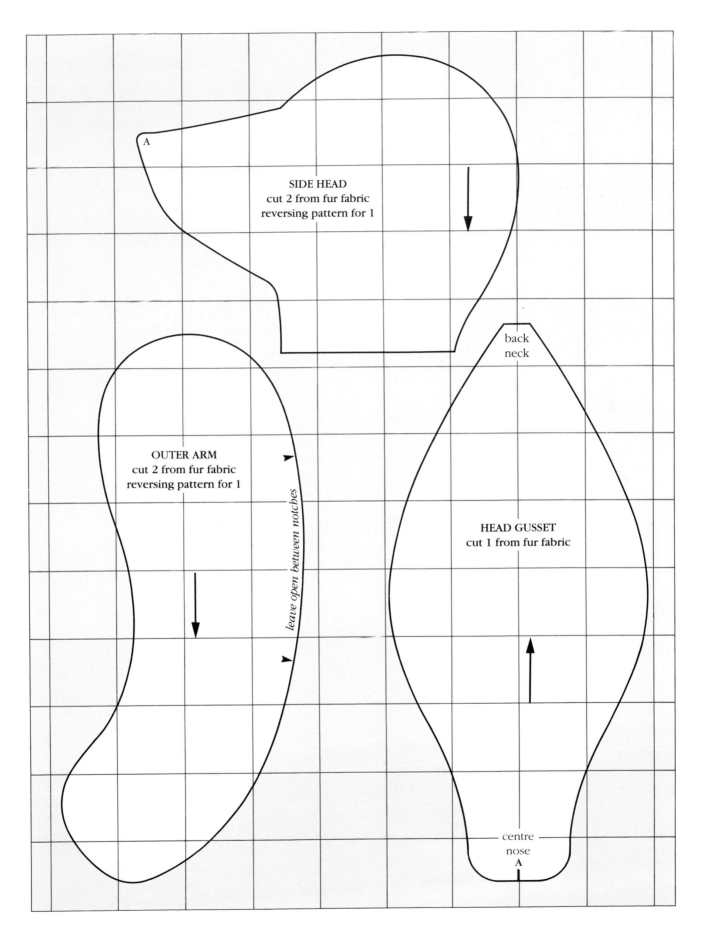

A

SIDE HEAD
cut 2 from fur fabric
reversing pattern for 1

back
neck

OUTER ARM
cut 2 from fur fabric
reversing pattern for 1

leave open between notches

HEAD GUSSET
cut 1 from fur fabric

centre
nose
A

1950s BRITISH BEAR

The bear pictured here was inspired by 1950s British bears. Made from gold fur fabric, it is 14in (36cm) tall and has dark chocolate brown pads.

Some of the most famous and early British bears came from the Chad Valley toy factory which began trading in that name in 1919. The company's origins are even earlier and date back to well before the turn of the century. However, Chad Valley teddy bears were not in full-time production until 1920.

Over the years, many soft toys were manufactured under the Chad Valley name but the most impressive must have been a range of large teddy bears which measured up to 28in (71cm). Chad Valley's advertisements proudly proclaimed that these bears were produced exclusively of British materials and were available in fabrics such as brown long beaver and best golden fur – the cheapest teddy in the range was described as an upright golden.

By the time World War II had ended and rationing across many countries had begun to subside, the 1950s had been ushered in along with a newer, brighter teddy. To begin with, its fur was probably of synthetic cotton-rayon rather than the more expensive mohair. Joints were cruder and several bear types had immovable limbs. The most important change in bears of this period was the introduction of the lock-in safety eyes, first patented by Wendy Boston for her washable bears of 1948.

Wendy Boston was one of the most renowned teddy bear producers of the 1950s. Her designs were usually unjointed and stuffed with kapok for a soft teddy.

Merrythought, of course, was another manufacturer of some note. During the 1950s, the company came up with the Cheeky bears range. These bears have broad faces, velvet noses and safety eyes.

It is also worth mentioning the Irish company, Gaeltarra Eireann or Tara Toys. This state-sponsored company began manufacturing bears shortly after World War II for export to Britain and the US, as well as the domestic market.

In Northern Ireland, the Pedigree factory was producing teddy bears by the end of the 1940s. Pedigree's other factory in Merton, known as the Triang works, was the other source of 1950s bears. Pedigree bears are very much the teddies of childhood – jointed limbs with brown velvet pads and glass eyes.

Lefray was the other British manufacturer of the day, producing traditional jointed gold and cinnamon bears with velvet pads.

Many bears from the 1920s onwards were stuffed with washed fleece. This makes a wonderful filling material, as it is hygienic, soft and easily worked. It is ideally suited for use with bears made from knitted fabrics, as it is less likely to distort the sewn shapes. Fleece should be used in the same way as kapok or polyester filling and can be bought from shops specializing in spinning requirements or by mail order from the suppliers listed on page 112.

MAKING THE 1950s BRITISH BEAR

Before starting to make the bear, carefully read the chapter on Classic Bear-making. Following the step-by-step instructions there, make the 8 templates, cut out the fabric pieces and assemble the bear, taking into consideration the special points below. Take care to keep your working surfaces as clean as possible at all times.

As the fabric used for this bear has a woven backing, great care must be taken when stitching and stuffing that it is not allowed to stretch and become mis-shapen. Tack (baste) all the seams carefully before machine stitching and do not over-stuff.

The felt front paws for this bear are stitched in position after the arms have been stuffed and closed. Use heavy-duty thread and tiny oversewing (overcasting) stitches to attach each paw, taking care to tease out any strands of pile which have been caught under the felt as you work.

The eyes are off-set slightly from the head gusset seam, so that their lower edges are about ⅞in (22mm) from the centre of the tip of the teddy bear's nose.

The ears should be set across the head gusset seams on top of the head, about 2in (5cm) apart. Do experiment with alternative positions, using 'T' pins to anchor the bear's ears in place, until you are satisfied with the results.

Trim the fur around the nose tip slightly, before working a small triangular nose in horizontal satin stitches, following the seamline at the tip of the muzzle for guidance. The mouth is then formed as an inverted 'T' from the tip of the triangle, using two strands of pearl cotton embroidery thread.

Materials

½yd (45cm) of 54in (137cm) wide gold acrylic fur fabric

Small square of dark chocolate brown felt

Tacking (basting) thread

Matching sewing thread

Matching heavy-duty thread

One 1⅜in (36mm) hardboard crown joint

Four 1in (25mm) hardboard crown joints

1lb (450g) natural fleece or polyester filling (stuffing)

Two ½in (12mm) amber glass eyes

One skein black 'pearl cotton' embroidery thread

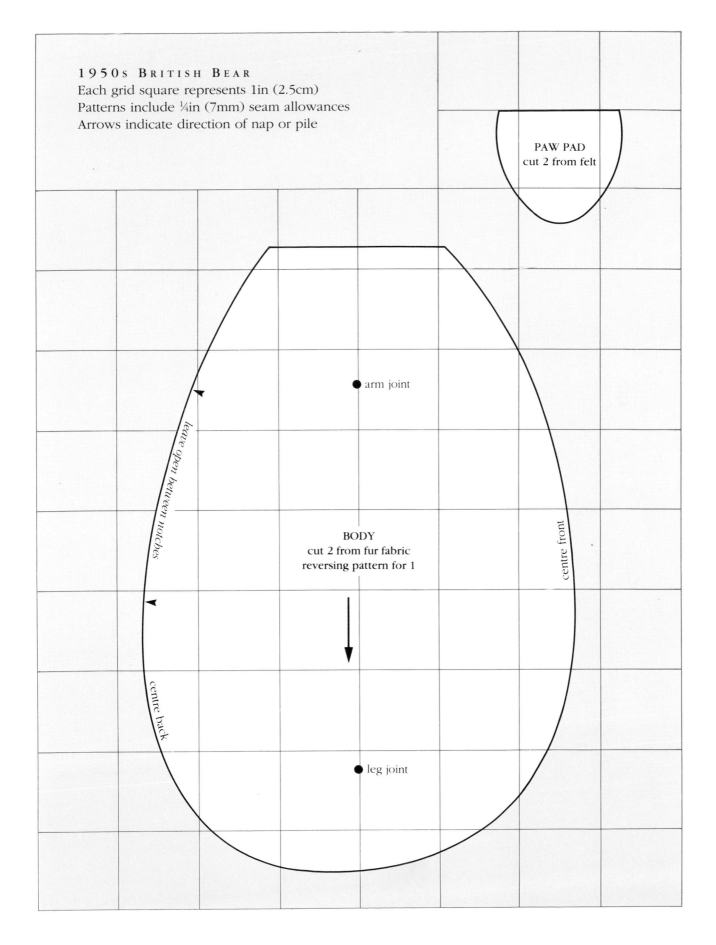

1950s BRITISH BEAR
Each grid square represents 1in (2.5cm)
Patterns include ¼in (7mm) seam allowances
Arrows indicate direction of nap or pile

PAW PAD
cut 2 from felt

● arm joint

leave open between notches

centre front

BODY
cut 2 from fur fabric
reversing pattern for 1

centre back

● leg joint

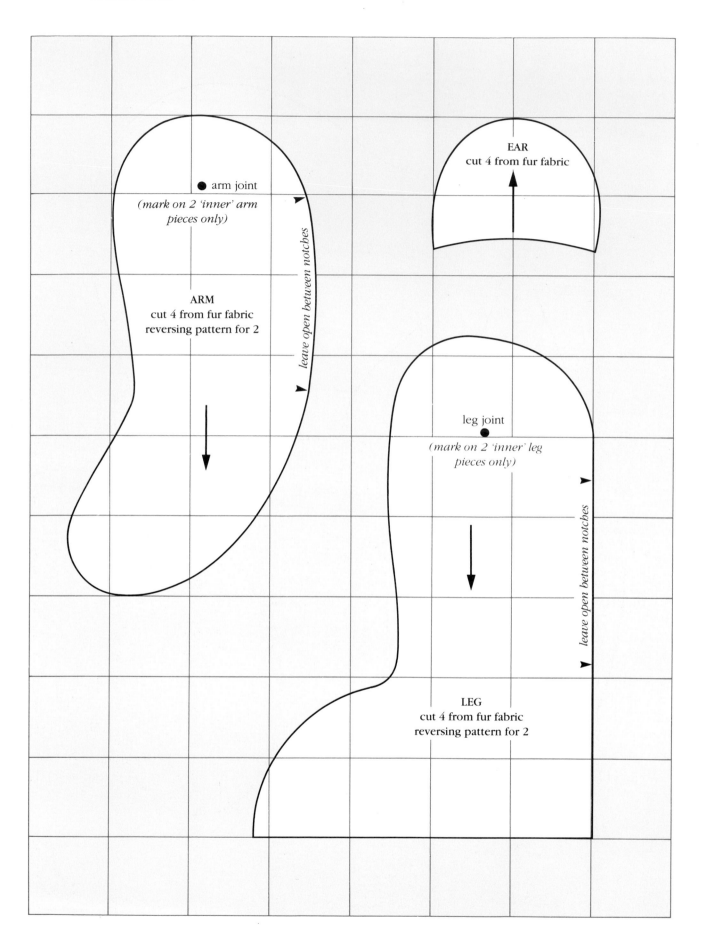

● arm joint

*(mark on 2 'inner' arm
pieces only)*

ARM
cut 4 from fur fabric
reversing pattern for 2

leave open between notches

EAR
cut 4 from fur fabric

leg joint

*(mark on 2 'inner' leg
pieces only)*

leave open between notches

LEG
cut 4 from fur fabric
reversing pattern for 2

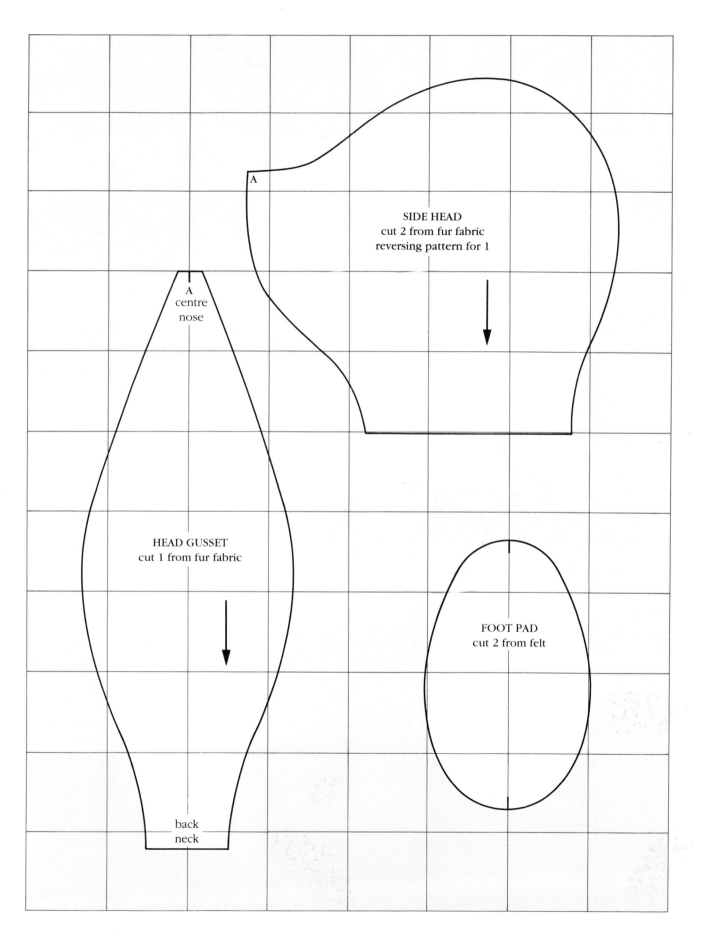

A

SIDE HEAD
cut 2 from fur fabric
reversing pattern for 1

A
centre
nose

HEAD GUSSET
cut 1 from fur fabric

FOOT PAD
cut 2 from felt

back
neck

1980s BEAR

The bear pictured here was inspired by 1980s bears. Made from honeysuckle mohair pile fabric, it is 9½in (24cm) tall and has dark brown velvet pads.

In all his ninety years of life, the teddy bear has never been more popular than he is now in the 1990s. Despite the coming of high technology and electronic gadgetry the traditional teddy bear still wins everyone's heart.

Teddy bears themselves have not escaped this new age though. Teddy bears are now often equipped with hidden tape cassettes so that they can speak or play music.

Television has had a large influence on new characters: Rupert Bear and Winnie-the-Pooh have been around since the 1920s, but are still much watched. Toys of these characters are also produced in abundance. More recently, characters like Paddington Bear, the creation of author Michael Bond, SuperTed and Teddy Ruxpin have been viewed by millions.

However, many modern bears were not living up to the success of their ancestors. Cheaper exports from the Far East caused many toy manufacturers to close because they simply could not keep up with the competition. The Australian teddy bear industry, for example, died in the 1970s because of this economic pressure.

It was the traditional bear that many people sought and companies like the Knickerbocker Toy Company and Steiff discovered that now was the time to bring the classic bears back. Since the early 1980s, Steiff have begun to produce replicas of the antique bears. The new bears still carry a Steiff button, but this is larger than the original one, as well as a Steiff label.

Firms like Dean's Co Ltd (Dean's Rag Book Co Ltd) began to market a range of reproduction jointed bears. The House of Nisbet introduced their Childhood Classics range of bears, Bully Bear being modelled on a bear from Peter Bull's collection (Peter Bull was an English actor, renowned for his love of bears).

Many other companies produced replica bears, often made with new materials which give a softer feel. Because classic bears are now so sought after and therefore very expensive, many teddy bear collectors are looking to replica bears as one way of assembling a range of classics without spending an absolute fortune.

Modern bears based on classic designs have certainly found a place in

the market. Unlike replica bears, these teddies have all the hallmarks of a well-designed, jointed bear, but are not strictly based on any previous model. These bears are often made from the finest materials and may even possess a range of accessories like scarves, hats or boots.

This 1980s bear is sporting a pair of tiny round spectacles, giving it a studious academic look. Equipped with a little knitted muffler in college or university colours, it would be an ideal gift for a student or graduate.

This small, rotund bear has dark brown velvet paws, which contrast nicely with its honeysuckle-coloured fur. Alternatively, a light beige or mushroom fabric could be used.

Materials

¼yd (25cm) of 54in (137cm) wide honeysuckle mohair with ⅜in (9mm) pile

Small square of dark brown velvet

Tacking (basting) thread

Matching sewing thread

Matching heavy-duty thread

One 1⅜in (36mm) hardboard crown joint

Four 1in (25mm) hardboard crown joints

8oz (230g) 'firm-fill' polyester filling (stuffing)

Two ⅜in (9mm) black boot button eyes

One skein black 'stranded cotton' embroidery thread

Small pair of gold-rimmed glasses (optional)

MAKING THE 1980s BEAR

Before starting to make up the bear, carefully read the chapter on Classic Bear-making. Following the step-by-step instructions there, make the 10 templates, cut out the fabric pieces and assemble the bear, taking into consideration the special points below. Seam allowances should be kept to a minimum – about ³⁄₁₆in (5mm).

The paw and foot pads for this bear have been cut from velvet. Use very small, even tacking (basting) stitches and pull out any trapped pile before machine stitching the paw pad to the inner arm section. Use the same technique to sew inner and outer arm sections together, leaving the tacking (basting) stitches in place if possible.

The foot pads are quite tricky to machine accurately, so it may be best to backstitch by hand over the tacking (basting) stitches using heavy-duty thread. The tacking (basting) stitches can then be left in, giving extra strength to the seam.

The eyes are placed on the head gusset seam, so that their lower edges are ¾in (2cm) from the nose tip.

The extra large ears should be set vertically on the head, the upper edge just touching the head gusset seam about 3in (8cm) from the tip of the nose.

Clip the fur back lightly around the muzzle before embroidering the nose, using short horizontal satin stitches to form a small rectangle. An inverted 'T' then forms the mouth which is worked using six strands of the stranded embroidery thread.

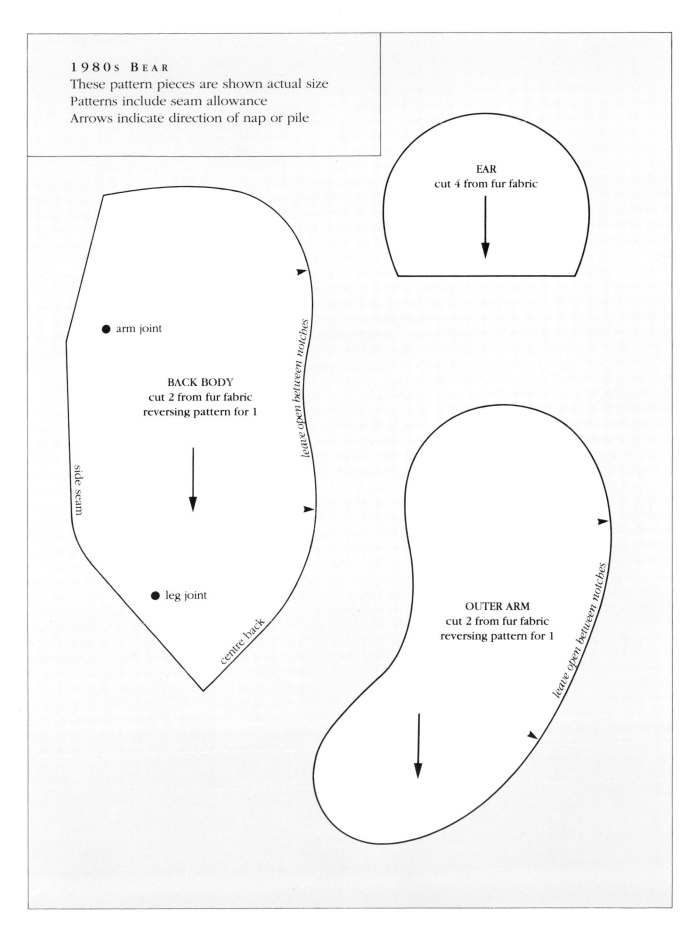

1980s Bear
These pattern pieces are shown actual size
Patterns include seam allowance
Arrows indicate direction of nap or pile

EAR
cut 4 from fur fabric

arm joint

BACK BODY
cut 2 from fur fabric
reversing pattern for 1

leave open between notches

side seam

leg joint

centre back

OUTER ARM
cut 2 from fur fabric
reversing pattern for 1

leave open between notches

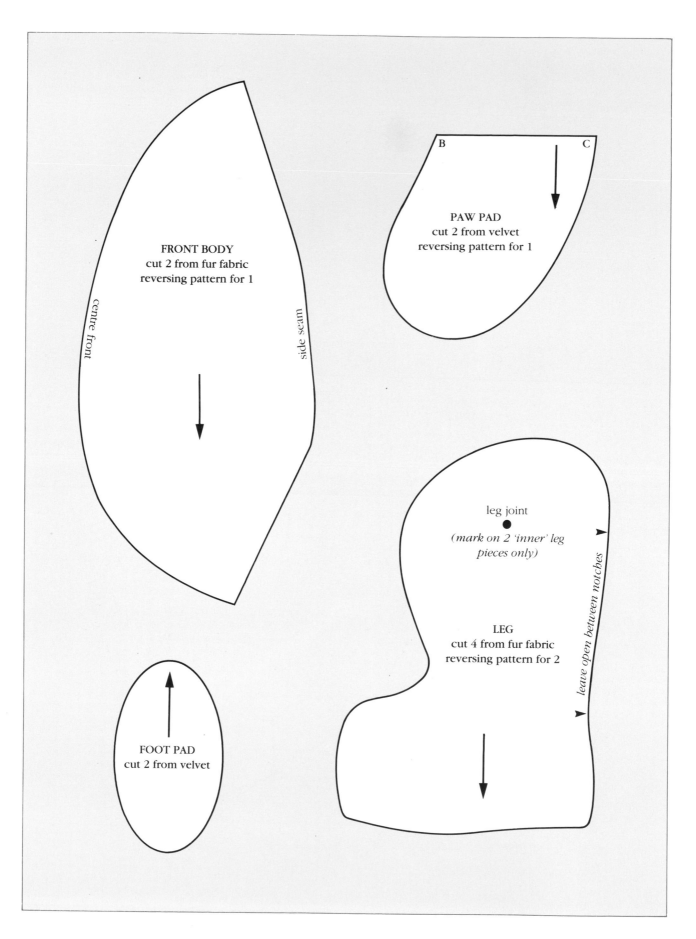

FRONT BODY
cut 2 from fur fabric
reversing pattern for 1

centre front

side seam

PAW PAD
cut 2 from velvet
reversing pattern for 1

B

C

leg joint
*(mark on 2 'inner' leg
pieces only)*

LEG
cut 4 from fur fabric
reversing pattern for 2

leave open between notches

FOOT PAD
cut 2 from velvet

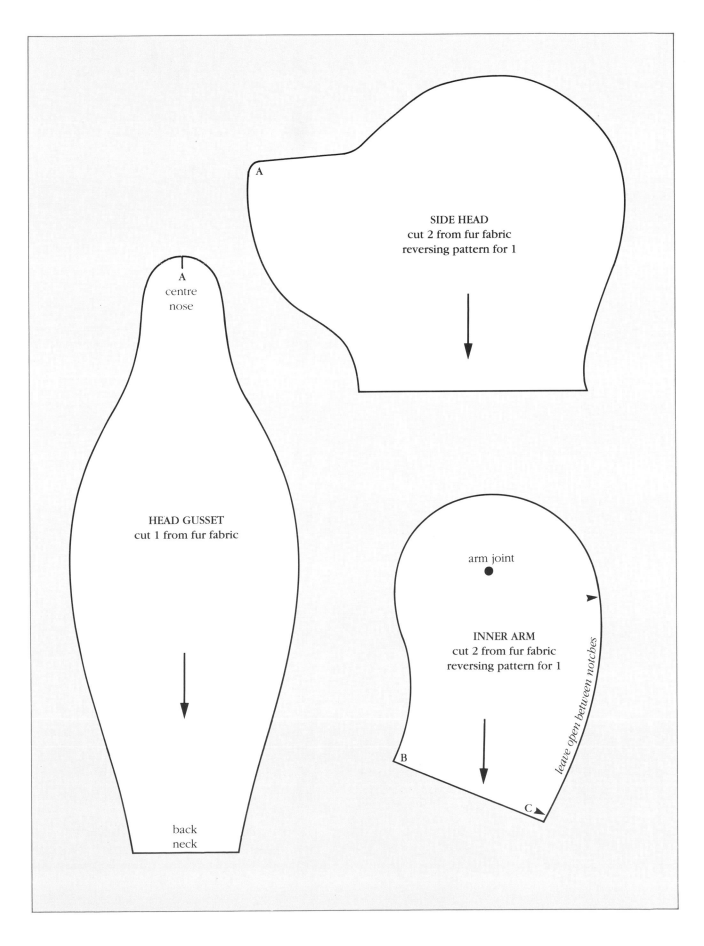

A

SIDE HEAD
cut 2 from fur fabric
reversing pattern for 1

A
centre
nose

HEAD GUSSET
cut 1 from fur fabric

arm joint

INNER ARM
cut 2 from fur fabric
reversing pattern for 1

leave open between notches

B

C

back
neck

MODERN BEAR

The bear pictured here is a version of a modern bear. Made from honey-beige distressed pile mohair fabric, it is 14in (36cm) tall and has pale beige suedette pads.

Is there a typical modern bear? With so many varieties of teddy on the market, it is almost impossible to define.

In the 1970s, cheap toys from the Far East put many Western manufacturers out of business. Certainly, the Australian industry, which had experienced a notable resurgence in the 1950s, could not compete, and teddy bear manufacturers in the country were just about wiped out.

However, with the craving for nostalgia, the classic bear has – since the 1980s – made something of a revival. Today, many companies in various countries produce traditional style bears from the highest quality materials with 'boot button' eyes and mohair fabric.

Traditional producers like Steiff and Merrythought quickly saw how this demand could be exploited and both companies now manufacture a successful line in replica bears – faithful reproductions of popular early teddy bears. These teddy bears are usually produced in a limited number and are made principally for the growing teddy bear collectors' market.

Teddy bear collecting in the United States and in Great Britain is experiencing something of a boom and interest is also strong in Germany and Japan. The widening availability of a large range of traditional mohair, cashmere and silk fabrics through mail order outlets and interest in teddy bear memorabilia has ensured that this interest should continue.

So great has been the revival of interest in classic teddy bears that many artists and craftsworkers have ventured into the field, producing distinctive bears, both classic and modern.

Generally, modern manufactured teddies display the most appealing characteristics from bears over a number of periods. However, the short, plump arms and legs give the modern bear a chubbier appearance. The modern bear's ears are also slightly padded to give the face an eager and inquiring look.

If you wish to experiment with your own style of bear, it is possible to adapt pieces from the various patterns in this book to create your own designs. By drawing the pattern shapes onto plain paper, it is possible to get an idea of how a finished bear might look by

*A 1990s Big Softies bear
called Marmaduke.*

Materials

*½yd (45cm) of 54in (137cm)
 wide honey-beige distressed
 pile mohair with ½in
 (12mm) pile
Small square of pale beige
 suedette
Tacking (basting) thread
Matching sewing thread
Matching heavy-duty thread
One 2in (50mm) hardboard
 crown joint
Four 1⅜in (36mm)
 hardboard crown joints
Small amount of firm-fill
 polyester filling (stuffing)
1lb (500g) wood wool
Two ½in (12mm) black glass
 boot button eyes
One skein black 'pearl cotton'
 embroidery thread*

assembling these paper templates. With a little practice it becomes quite easy to gauge accurately the effect achieved by substituting a different ear shape or a thinner or longer arm.

It is a good idea, until you are confident in your abilities, to cut your experimental bear from a cheaper fabric. An inexpensive acrylic fabric is useful for testing on, even though it is slightly stretchier. Any adaptations and alterations can be made on the prototype bear at little cost until you achieve the type of bear that appeals most. This can be great fun and the result is a unique and totally individual creation.

The modern bear here has a cuddly, round body and an unusual but endearing expression. It has been made from a honey-beige, long-pile mohair and just longs to be hugged! Mohair can be obtained in a range of dramatic colours, including royal blue, purple and red, and this modern bear could be made in any of these shades – the choice is yours.

MAKING THE MODERN BEAR

Before starting to make the bear, carefully read the chapter on Classic Bear-making. Following the step-by-step instructions there, make the 10 templates, cut out the fabric pieces and assemble the bear, taking into consideration the special points below. Take care to keep your working surfaces as clean as possible at all times.

Fill the muzzle firmly with polyester filling (stuffing) before continuing to stuff the head with wood wool. Stuff the body very firmly using wood wool with some polyester stuffing, if necessary, taking care to pack out the upper back to form a definite hump on the bear.

The eyes are placed just below the head gusset seam, so that their lower edges are 1⅜in (3.5cm) from the tip of the muzzle.

Before attaching the ears, pad them out slightly using a tiny amount of polyester filling. Taking care when sewing them in position, that strand of the filling do not become entangled with the stitching. The ears should be set towards the back of the head across the gusset seams and about 2½in (6cm) apart.

The triangular nose is worked in horizontal satin stitches over the tip of the head gusset.

From the tip of the nose triangle, the thread is doubled and two vertical straight stitches about 1in (2.5cm) in length are made following the centre seam of the lower muzzle. From the lower point of the straight stitches, still keeping the thread doubled, a smiling mouth is formed by stitching two straight stitches at an angle to left and right.

The fur pile around the nose and mouth can be trimmed away slightly, just to tidy up the muzzle if necessary.

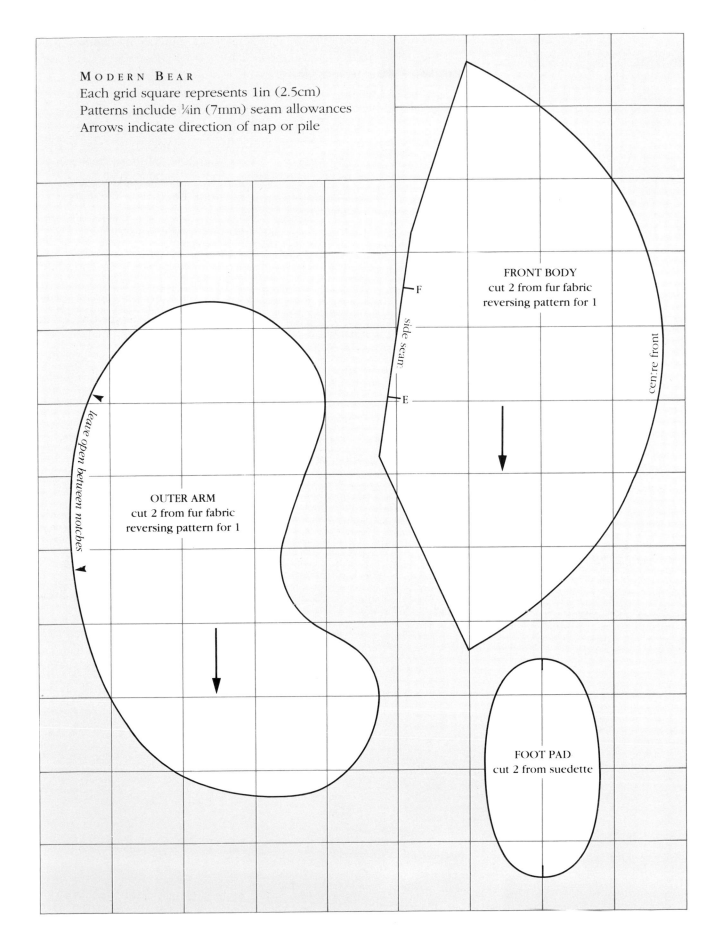

MODERN BEAR
Each grid square represents 1in (2.5cm)
Patterns include ¼in (7mm) seam allowances
Arrows indicate direction of nap or pile

FRONT BODY
cut 2 from fur fabric
reversing pattern for 1

side seam

F

E

centre front

OUTER ARM
cut 2 from fur fabric
reversing pattern for 1

leave open between notches

FOOT PAD
cut 2 from suedette

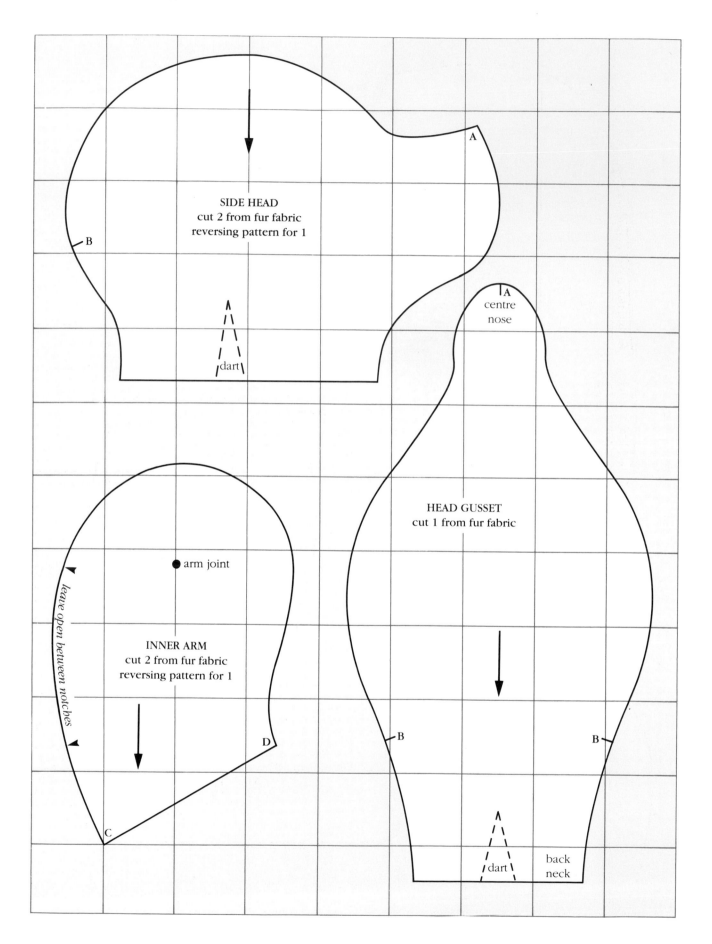

SIDE HEAD
cut 2 from fur fabric
reversing pattern for 1

B

A

dart

A
centre
nose

HEAD GUSSET
cut 1 from fur fabric

arm joint

leave open between notches

INNER ARM
cut 2 from fur fabric
reversing pattern for 1

D

B

B

C

dart

back
neck

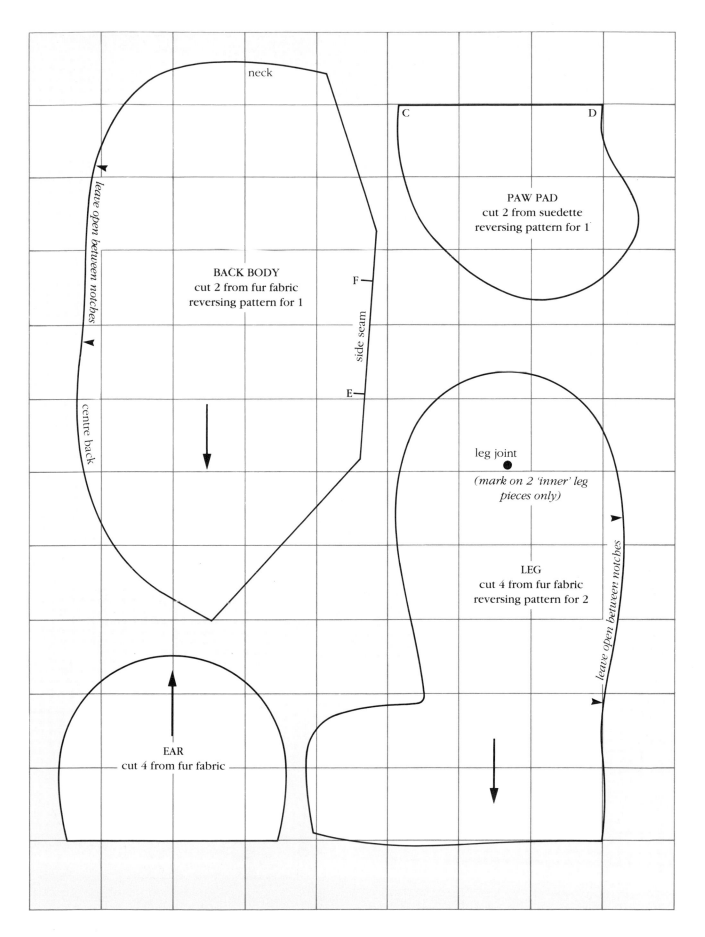

neck

C   D

PAW PAD
cut 2 from suedette
reversing pattern for 1

leave open between notches

BACK BODY
cut 2 from fur fabric
reversing pattern for 1

centre back

F

side seam

E

leg joint

*(mark on 2 'inner' leg
pieces only)*

LEG
cut 4 from fur fabric
reversing pattern for 2

leave open between notches

EAR
cut 4 from fur fabric

USEFUL ADDRESSES

Author
Julia Jones' Collectors' Bears,
PO Box 16, Swadlincote,
Derbyshire DE12 8ZZ, Great Britain.
*For specially commissioned bears. Also
after-dinner speaking engagements
and illustrated lectures.*

Bear supplies
*For fabrics and/or bear components
and stuffings contact the following:*

Oakley Fabrics Ltd, 8 May Street,
Luton, Beds LU1 3QY, Great Britain.
Tel: 0582 424828. Fax: 0582 29362.
(Mail order supplies worldwide)

Nonsuch Soft Toys, 51 Dudley Close,
Tilehurst, Reading, Berkshire RG3 6JJ,
Great Britain. Tel: 0734 413006.
(Mail order available)

Bridon Bears of Cheltenham,
2 St Margaret's Terrace, Cheltenham,
Glos GL50 4DT, Great Britain.
Tel: 0242 513102.
(Mail order available)

Animal Crackers, 5824 Isleta,
Albuquerque, NM 87105-6628, USA.
Tel: (505) 873 2806.

Golden Fun, Box 10697-TBF, Golden,
CO 80401-0600, USA.

Carver's Eye Company, Dept 60,
PO Box 16692, Portland, OR 97216,
USA. Tel: (503) 666 5680.

Spare Bear Parts, PO Box 56F,
Interlochen, MI 49643, USA.
Tel: (616) 275 6993.
Fax: (616) 275 6230.

Bear Clawset, 27 Palermo Walk,
Long Beach, CA 90803, USA.
Tel: (310) 434 8077.

Bear charity
Good Bears of the World (UK)
Tel: 081 891 5746.

Toy safety information
British Standards Institute,
Linford Wood, Milton Keynes,
MK14 6LE, Great Britain.
Tel: 0908 220022. Fax: 320 856.

Publications
The Teddy Bear Times, Heritage Press,
Shelley House, 104 High Street,
Steyning, West Sussex BN4 3RD,
Great Britain.

The UK Teddy Bear Guide and Teddy
Bear Magazine, Hugglets, PO Box 290,
Brighton, West Sussex BN2 1DR,
Great Britain.

Teddy Bear and Friends Magazines,
Cumberland Publishing, Inc.,
900 Frederick Street, Cumberland,
Maryland 21502, USA.
Tel: (301) 759-5853.
Fax: (301) 759-9108.

Teddy bear clubs
British Teddy Bear Association,
PO Box 290, Brighton, West Sussex
BN2 1DR, Great Britain.
Tel: 0273 697974.
Fax: 0273 62655.

Teddy Ecosse, The Wynd, Melrose,
Roxburghshire, Scotland TD6 9PA.

International League of Teddy Bear
Collectors Club, c/o 1023 Don Diablo,
Arcadia, California 91006, USA.
Tel: (818) 447 3809.

Teddy's Patch, Le Club des Amis de
l'Ours, 34 Rue Lieu de Santé, 76000
Rouen, France.
Tel: 35 88 96 00.

Associations and guilds
British Toymakers Guild,
124 Walcot Street, Bath, Avon
BA1 5BG, Great Britain.
Tel: 0225 442440.

Teddy Bear Traders Association,
c/o Gerry Grey, The Old Bakery
Teddy Bear Shop, 38 Cambridge Street,
Wellingborough, Northants NN8 1DW,
Great Britain.
Tel: 0933 229191.
Fax: 0933 272466.

Museums with bear collections
Bethnal Green Museum of Childhood,
Cambridge Heath Road, London
E2 9PA, Great Britain.
Tel: 081 981 1711.

The Bear Museum, 38 Dragon Street,
Petersfield, Hants GU31 4JJ, Great
Britain. Tel: 0730 265108.

Pollock's Toy Museum, 1 Scala Street,
London W1P 1LT, Great Britain.
Tel: 071 636 3452.

The Teddy Bear Museum, 19 Greenhill
Street, Stratford-upon-Avon CV37 6LF,
Great Britain. Tel: 0789 293160.

The Margaret Woodbury Strong
Museum, Rochester, New York, USA.

Margarete Steiff Museum, Giengen,
Germany.

Romy's Bazaar, 2 Badgery's Crescent,
Lawson 2783, Australia.

Auctions
*Classic Bears are sometimes featured in
sales held by auctioneers Christies and
Sotheby's. For information contact
main offices in London or New York.*

ACKNOWLEDGEMENTS
The Author would like to thank the
following for their immense help, both
practical and material, in the
researching and writing of this book:
Roy Pilkington of Oakley Fabrics;
Alastair McMinn and Donald McMillan
of Coats Patons Crafts; David Fish of
Tootal; Kath Mason of Mason Bears;
Bridon Bears of Cheltenham; David
and Susan Rixon of Nonsuch Bears
and Mr and Mrs Wharnsby of Good
Bears of the World.

Special thanks to Jon Stewart for the
photography and Kate Yeates of Anaya
Publishers, Alison Leach and Clare
Clements for their editorial and design
skills and finally to my brother and
sister- in-law, Roger and Pam Smith,
for their continuing encouragement
and support.

PICTURE CREDITS
The publishers would like to thank
The Bear Museum, Petersfield for use
of photos on pages 44, 50, 60, 66, 78
and 90; and The Teddy Bear Museum,
Stratford-upon-Avon for use of photos
on pages 1, 6 and 108.